# A GUIDE TO THE BAY AREA'S BEST ETHNIC RESTAURANTS

## 1990 EDITION

### RICHARD & LINDA FLAMM

ZORBA PRESS
ALEXANDER LAKE, CONNECTICUT

A Guide To The Bay Area's Best Ethnic Restaurants--Or How To Travel Around The World Without Leaving San Francisco. Copyright © 1989 by Richard and Linda Flamm. All rights reserved. No portion of this book may be reproduced in any form whatsoever without written permission from the publisher. Address permission and bulk order inquiries to: Zorba Press West, P.O. Box 8224, Berkeley, California 94707.

Printed in the United States of America.
First published October 1989.

Library of Congress Catalog Card Number: 89-51203
ISBN: 0-927379-77-5

Cover Design and All Illustrations: Linda Flamm
Director of Book Production: Michael Pastore

10 9 8 7 6 5 4 3 2 1

# CONTENTS

Introduction ................................. 5

How To Use This Book ..................... 9

1    England and Ireland ................... 11

2    Central and Northern Europe ............ 21
*Denmark • Germany • Holland • Sweden • Switzerland*

3    Southern Europe ...................... 31
*Basque Region • Greece • Portugal • Spain*

4    Eastern Europe ....................... 47
*Czechoslovakia • Hungary • Poland • Russia • Yugoslavia*

5    The Middle East ...................... 59
*Afghanistan • Armenia • Lebanon • Persia • Turkey*

6    Africa ............................... 71
*Algeria • Egypt • Eritrea • Ethiopia • Morocco • Tunisia*

7    India ................................ 87

8    Southeast Asia ....................... 117
*Burma • Cambodia • Laos*

9    The Pacific Rim ...................... 129
*Australia • Indonesia • Korea • The Philippines*

10   Central and South America ............. 151
*Brazil • Cuba • El Salvador • Haiti • Jamaica • Nicaragua • Peru • Puerto Rico*

Appendix A: Restaurants Not Yet Reviewed ... 169

Appendix B: Glossary of Ethnic Food Terms .. 179

Index of Restaurants ...................... 187

## INTRODUCTION

Properly seen, all of life is a travel and travel--more than anything else--is a state of mind. If you are a fellow traveller, you probably know what we mean. If not, let us try to explain: there is a joy one gets from travelling that is quite unlike anything else on Earth. Travelling, *really* travelling, makes you feel like a wide-eyed child again--eager and innocent--awed by all that your senses are attempting, sometimes vainly, to drink in.

For many, the pay back comes upon the return trip home. As the joy of newness and continuous revelation slowly gives way to the torpor and sameness of day to day life in the U.S.A, one is apt to sink into a state of profound melancholy. Sometimes it almost makes you not want to travel, knowing how low you're bound to feel on that return trip home.

We are well aware that one pays a price for experiencing the joy of travel, but we still love it. Only now that we're older and, like most people our age, saddled with responsibilities, we find we don't have the time or energy to pick up and jot about the globe. We learned long ago, however, that just because you can't hop on a plane doesn't mean you can't travel at all.

At that time, we lived in New York. We would often marvel at all the French and Japanese tourists strolling down Fifth Avenue, merrily clicking their Konicas; and we'd think to ourselves that we would probably feel the same way if we were strolling in the Ginza or down the Champs Elysées. After all, virtually every place one can travel is home to somebody else; and, conversely, our home--for others--may be a glorious adventure. But how can one capture the spirit of adventure without actually leaving home?

What we used to do was take "mini-travels". Across the East River from Manhattan is Astoria--sometimes called the "third city of Greece" after Salonika and Athens. We'd simply hop on a subway and, in minutes, be transported into a neighborhood which--while maybe only a couple of miles away--might as well have been on the other side of the world. After downing a big glass of *ouzo* (a Greek liqueur) at a local "taverna" and a hearty meal at an authentic Greek restaurant--and after an entire evening of hearing nothing but Greek conversation, laughter and song--we'd come away feeling as rejuvenated and refreshed as if we'd just spent an evening in the shadow of the Parthenon itself.

We soon got into the habit of taking off on one of these adventures at every opportunity. On one day we would pop onto the "path" train to Newark's "Ironbound" district--America's answer to Lisbon. The next day we might head for the Russian or Middle Eastern sections of Brooklyn. After awhile, we came to see our visits to these places as being similar in purpose, if not in scope, to a travel abroad.

While the Big Apple is, of course, America's ethnic capital, the nation's other "B.A."--the Bay Area--is fast becoming number two. There may be no Astorias or Ironbounds here, but there are literally thousands of ethnic restaurants. In fact, for some ethnicities, most notably those from Southeast Asia and the Far East, there is far more "travelling" to be done here than even in New York.

This having been said, a word of explanation is in order. In compiling this guide, certain parameters had to be set. For us to attempt to review every Bay Area restaurant representing a foreign country would be a hopeless task, and one which would certainly dilute the book's value as a guide. Rather than do this, we realized we would have to make some "cuts". This, however, did not turn out to be as subjective or as difficult as we had at first anticipated it might be.

Restaurants representing countries such as China, France and Italy, in particular, have become so common throughout most of the United States--so completely dissolved into the American "melting pot"-- that, for all intents and purposes, they cannot properly be thought of as exotic, or perhaps even "ethnic", anymore.

Other types of restaurants--such as Japanese, Mexican, Vietnamese and Thai--might still be considered a novelty in other parts of the country, but not here. Since it would be impractical to include all foreign restaurants within the scope of this book, we have opted not to include restaurants from any of these more familiar destinations.

Finally, what this book isn't. This book isn't designed to tell you where a particular chef studied cooking, what a sommelier thinks the most suitable wine is, or what coupons or discounts a restaurant might happen to offer. It also isn't intended to be a guide to the Bay Area's cheapest restaurants, the ones that stay open the latest, or the ones most likely to be out of business before the next edition of this book appears. In other words, while in form this book may appear to be a typical restaurant guide, in our view it is a *travel* guide. So, whereas a typical restaurant critic might be apt to conclude this introduction by wishing you "bon appetit", we prefer to send you off with a hale and hardy "bon voyage".

---Richard and Linda Flamm, Berkeley California

# HOW TO USE THIS BOOK

Every restaurant we visit is rated on a 20 point scale, 10 for "atmosphere"--which includes all those elements that go into one's subjective impression of the restaurant such as decor, service, and music--and 10 for quality of cuisine. In our reviews, a restaurant's atmosphere score is shown first, followed by its rating for cuisine and a composite. For example, EL OSO (Spain) (9/10=19) means that the restaurant El Oso, which specializes in Spanish cuisine, received an extremely good "9" for ambience, and a perfect "10" for cuisine.

For restaurants whose combined totals fall below the average of their peers (less than "10") the symbol (n/r), meaning "no rating", is indicated. Even though for such restaurants no score is shown, basic information about them--e.g. hours and credit cards accepted--is still provided. (Credit cards are denoted by the following symbols: V--Visa, MC--Master Card, AE--American Express and DC--Diner's Club). Note that the fact that a restaurant receives a "no rating" from us does not necessarily mean it is no good. Rather, this may merely indicate that, in our view, the restaurant is not a particularly authentic exponent of the culture it purports to represent.

"Appendix A" contains a list of ethnic restaurants not reviewed in this edition. There are many reasons why a restaurant might not have been reviewed, and no judgment as to its ambience or quality of cuisine should be ascribed to the fact that it appears in Appendix A rather than in the main body of the text. It could be that the restaurant is new, was temporarily closed on our last visit, has not yet been visited by us, or was reviewed too late to be included in this edition.

"Appendix B" is a selected glossary of some common ethnic food terms used in this book. It is not meant to be exhaustive, but is intended only to help the reader familiarize her or himself with a vast array of ethnic foods at a glance.

Finally, as every avid ethnic restaurant-goer knows, new restaurants continuously crop up while others close, and many of the ones which do survive and flourish occasionally change ownership, chefs, decor or menus. This fact makes keeping on top of the Bay Area ethnic restaurant scene both challenging and, at times, frustrating.

In an effort to maintain the most accurate information possible, we solicit your help. If you think we missed a restaurant we should know about, if you had a particularly good or bad dining experience, or if there is anything else you think we should know but don't, please write to us care of Zorba Press West at P.O. Box 8224, Berkeley CA 94707. Thanks!

ENGLAND

IRELAND

## 1. ENGLAND AND IRELAND

The odyssey of most round-the-world travellers begins with a visit to either England or Ireland. In terms of language and culture the transition is easy, and the same holds true for the food. While the Brits are often criticized for the lack of diversity of their fare (Somerset Maugham once quipped that to dine well in England one has to eat breakfast three times a day), there are at least four different types of English and/or Irish restaurants in the Bay Area. First, there are "traditional" English places. These tend to be fairly formal and serve "serious" entrees like *beef Wellington*--beef baked in a puff pastry, and *roast beef and Yorkshire pudding*--the latter being a dumpling-like concoction made with flour, milk and eggs. They may also offer some tempting desserts such as *trifle*-- pound cake and fruits, sometimes soaked in sherry and topped with custard and whipped cream, or *bread pudding*.

A second type of English eatery, much beloved by Yanks, is the pub. In addition to a plethora of lagers, ales and beers, pubs serve a limited slate of simple, but hearty fare of generally good quality and moderate price. Standard "pub grub" offerings include *Cornish pasties* (pronounced "pass-tees")--turnovers stuffed with meat or potatoes; *bangers and mash*- -fried beef or pork sausages served with mashed potatoes; and *shepherd's pie*--a delightful minced meat and potato casserole. Another popular British innovation--the English answer to the hot dog--is *fish and chips*. "F & C", as it is known in the Isles, consists of a generous portion of fried cod, usually doused in tangy malt vinegar, served with a healthy portion of french fries. While in England F & C is normally served in shops devoted to making good F & C and nothing else, here you are likely to be offered F & C in pubs.

Then there are British tea rooms. These tend to be "proper" but casual--their dignified nature seldom being reflected by inordinately high prices. While there is no standard tea room bill of fare, some items common to many are *scones*--crisp hot buttered rolls; *clotted cream*--made from standing milk over hot water until the cream solidifies and can be skimmed; *finger sandwiches*, often made with cucumbers or cheese; and *welsh rarebit*--cheddar cheese mixed with beer, then grilled on toast.

Finally, you may come across the odd Irish Bar and Grill. These tend to be imbued with a fun-loving air reflective of the often boisterous and seemingly always gregarious nature of the Irish people themselves. Many Irish Bars feature live music, and sure if there won't also be some splendid fare--such as *corned beef and cabbage* or creamy white *Irish stew*--made with mutton, potatoes and onions. Some solid Irish dessert possibilities include *baked custard, Irish Cream pie,* and *spotted dog*--a spiced raisin bread pudding served with whiskey sauce.

## STANLEY'S {Ireland/England} (9/10=19)

2369 S. Winchester Bl. Campbell (408) 378-6484

Although few people outside the San Jose area seem to know about it, Stanley's--an ornate Irish bar located in a nondescript Campbell shopping center--has been serving up great Irish and English fare at reasonable prices for some time. It used to offer what was, hands down, the Bay Area's best Sunday brunch, featuring all sorts of scrumptious British and Irish dishes you could never find anywhere else. Alas, those days are gone. Stanley's is, however, still well worth going to, not only for its innovative and reasonably-priced food, but for its marvelously authentic Irish atmosphere, which peaks on Thursday nights when live Celtic music fills the room. Stanley's menu is extremely diverse, with something for everyone. Start with *musharroms frigassy* (no misprint--$3.95). This consists of mushrooms sauteed with herbs in a brown wine sauce (adapted from a 17th Century Celtic recipe). Many of Stanley's traditional beef dishes, such as *steak and kidney pie* ($9.95) and spiced *beef and cabbage* ($9.50), are better here than elsewhere; and there are some unique beef items on the menu as well, like *Lancer's steak'o'bob*--a brochette wrapped in rashers (Irish-style bacon) and lanced with onions and mushrooms ($11.95). We also like Stanley's *misty beef pie* ($9.95), which features sirloin strips and mushrooms sauteed in Irish Mist, then cooked in a cream sauce and served in a short crust pie. One of our favorite poultry dishes anywhere is Stanley's *cockie leekie pie*--a traditional Scottish recipe which features, predictably enough, chunks of chicken with leeks, as well as mushrooms, in a pastry shell ($9.95). Veal fans will find their manna in Stanley's *veal and oysters Galway*--a broiled veal steak topped with oysters sauteed in a sauce composed of spinach, Irish Mit and cream ($13.95). Seafood fanciers will want to consider retaining the *Dublin Lawyers*, lobster and mushrooms in a rich cream and Irish whiskey sauce ($22.95). Finally, pork enthusiasts will find happiness in *pig's rings*--cooked in a whiskey and chutney sauce ($9.95). At many English/Irish (or in this case, Irish/English) establishments, desserts are a forgettable afterthought but, at Stanley's, you better save some room. Its homemade *fruit cobblers*, *spotted dog* ($1.95) and Irish cream pie ($2.50) are out of this world. Despite its out of the way location, Stanley's is well worth going to. It may be one of the Bay Area's top twenty ethnic restaurants of any kind.

Hours: Tu-F 11:30-2:30; Tu-Su 5:30-9:30.
Cards: All major.

## THE ENGLISH ROSE {England} (9/8=17)

663 Laurel St. San Carlos 595-5549

When an ethnic restaurant makes you nostalgic for the country it represents, it must be doing something right. The English Rose makes us long for the British Isles in a way few other local shops do. Maybe it is the lace curtains or matching floral tablecloths and tea warmers (which really do the job). Maybe its the restaurant's fine china or all of its portraits and pictures of people and things associated with the Empire, such as a colorful poster extolling the virtues of Devon Tea. Whatever accounts for the feeling, the overall effect is true. While at tea shops like E.R. you won't find all the mainstays of the English diet, you will be able to experience some of them; including lemon curd, cornish pasties, and a nice *ploughman's lunch*--cheese, rolls, apples and chutney ($5.95). Your logical choice, however, is E.R.'s *teaplate*, which features a variety of *scones, crumpets* and *teabreads*. How good are E.R.'s offerings? Well, consider that owner/chef Marilyn Sheppard sells her own cookbook.

Hours: M-F 10-4; Sa 9-3.
Cards: No. But personal checks are accepted.

## PELICAN INN {England} (9/7=16)

Muir Beach 383-6000

A close to authentic re-creation of a 17th Century English Country Inn set in an appropriately pastoral setting complete with expansive lawns and horses. The Inn's quaint, even romantic, interior--with its low beamed ceiling and antique agricultural instruments--make one pine for a misty day in the Cumbrian dales. An outdoor patio is a pleasant place to partake of the Pelican's popular (but not particularly authentic) all-you-can-eat Sunday brunch, which features fresh cut roast beef, creamy potatoes and other fairly standard fare. While the Pelican's regular dinner menu includes several American items, there are some sound English choices as well, such as *beef Wellington*--beef baked in a puff pastry with goose liver pate ($15.95), and *Devonshire chicken*--sauteed breast of chicken in a sherry mustard sauce ($13.95). For our money, the best time to visit is at lunch when the Pelican offers a full slate of traditional British dishes at extremely reasonable prices ($5.00-$8.00).

Hours: Tu-Su 11:30-3; 6-9.
Cards: V/MC.

## MAYFLOWER INNE {England} (7/6=13)

1533 Fourth St.   San Rafael   456-1011

One of the Bay Area's more authentic pubs, the Mayflower boasts some eye-catching gewgaws like a suit of armor as well as more typical pub features like animated beer-fueled conversation and an oft-used dartboard. On weekends there are piano sing-alongs which, we are told, can get pretty wild. Recently, a kazoo and washboard performance by the "Dreadful Grates"--a group chosen at random from the audience--spilled out onto San Rafael's streets. Manager Trevor Riches got into the spirit by donning his London bobby's helmet and holding up traffic on Fourth Street to let the troop pass. (Unfortunately, among the passing cars was one manned by a couple of San Rafael's finest.) The Mayflower serves typical "pub grub" like *bangers and mash* and *shepherd's pie*, but these are not spectacular and, at $8.95, are a bit overpriced. We prefer the Inne's fish and chips. The hands down best thing on the menu, however, is homemade rhubarb pie ($2.00).

Hours: M-F 11:30-2:30; Daily 5-9.
Cards: MC/V.

## THE LONDON HOUSE {England} (6/6=12)

630 Ramona Ave.   Palo Alto   321-0778

The London House is an unusual place. Despite its billing as an "Elizabethan pub" and tea room, it somehow lacks the atmosphere of either a true British tea room or a true British pub. This is attributable, in part, to the fact that the restaurant doubles as a gift shop--its dining area being hedged in between shelves of British sundries such as Cadbury bars and Twinings teas. With cardigans and other Scottish woolens draped over the mezzanine, you feel more like you are dining in a British department store than in any sort of eatery. The London House does boast a few solid "British" specialties however, such as *Irish Guiness stew* ($8.95), braised lamb kidneys on toast ($3.95) and toasted crumpets with jam ($3.95); as well as an extensive list of genuine British lagers, ales and even *pub cider* (5% alcohol). The gift shop also stocks an impressive array of British goods, thus making the London House perhaps a better place to shop than to dine.

Hours: Tu & Sa 11-5; W & F 11-10.
Cards: MC/V.

## PENNY FARTHING PUB {England} (5/6=11)

679 Sutter St.   San Francisco   771-5155

Since there are not one, but two, Bay Area Penny Farthings, you might as well know what a "penny farthing" is. It is that peculiar form of British cycle with a large wheel in front and a small wheel in the rear. *This* Penny Farthing is probably the closest thing to a true British Pub anywhere near the financial district. Prices are reasonable, and the restaurant does boast several solid British offerings such as fish and chips in a homemade beer batter ($4.95); *shepherd's pie*--ground lamb casserole with mashed potatoes ($5.95); *steak and kidney pie* ($5.95); *sherry trifle*--sherry soaked pound cake and fruits topped with custard & whipped cream ($1.95); and *bread pudding*--baked with apples and raisins, served warm with brown sugar and bourbon sauce ($1.95). The problem is that the Penny Farthing also serves a number of American items such as a penny burger and even a Mexican chicken sandwich. A Mexican chicken sandwich in a British Pub?  No, no, no--we dare say.

Hours: Daily 11:30--11:30.
Cards: All major.

## ABIGAIL'S {England} (4/6=10)

265 N. First St.   San Jose   (408) 294-4111

Abigail's menu promises "a bit of British charm in the heart of downtown San Jose", and that's just what you get, a *bit* of England. Although inexplicably called a pub, Abigail's looks considerably more like a traditional British tea room, with elegant Victorian furnishings. It is also notable for the fact that the restaurant is set in the back of a florist's shop. There, however, any analogy to England ends. Abigail's music and decor are, for the most part, American; and even its menu is largely new world, with indigenous items such as California shrimp salad sharing the bill with more authentic ones like *grilled bangers and mash* ($5.95), *ploughman's lunch* ($4.95) and assorted fresh-baked British pies. If you happen to be in downtown San Jose, Abigail's is a pretty good place to go for a cup of tea and some warm *scones*, or its large selection of British lagers and ales. It does not, however, warrant a special trip.

Hours: M-F 8:30-5; F-Sa 6-10; Su 10-2.
Cards: All major (except DC).

## KENSINGTON CIRCUS {England} (4/6=10)

389 Colusa Ave.  Kensington  524-8814

This attractive restaurant offers some interesting, traditional British items you may not be able to find elsewhere such as *bubble and squeak*--smoked turkey, cabbage and cheese in a potato cake ($8.50) and *toad in the hole*--grilled herb sausages in a beer batter with vegetables. Unfortunately, at least from an ethnic point of view, the restaurant places a premium on "California cuisine".

Hours: Daily. Pub: 5:30--12(m); Kitchen 5:30-9:30.
Cards: MC/V

## IRELAND'S 32 {Ireland} (n/r)

3920 Geary Blvd.  San Francisco  386-6173

A pool table dominates this somewhat authentic but not particularly inviting Irish Pub. Some genuine Irish dishes such as Irish Stew ($3.35) and Bread Pudding ($1.75) are available, but the best time to visit is at breakfast, when you have a choice of two Irish *fry's*: *Connaught*--eggs, bacon, sausage, black and white pudding and fries; or *Ulster*--same meats with black pudding, soda bread and potato bread (both $6.50).

Hours: M-F 12(n)-3(a), Sa-Su 1(p)-4(a).
Cards: AE/DC.

## B.J. BULL {England} (n/r)

3403 Alma Ave.  Palo Alto  493-7330

In the small Sierra town of Grass Valley there are not one, but three restaurants specializing in the tasty Cornish delights known as *pasties*. In the Bay Area proper, while a few British pubs serve pasties, no one specializes in them; no one, that is, except B.J. Bull. This quaint place--located about as far off the beaten track as you can go and still be in Palo Alto--lacks true British atmosphere, but doesn't lack for pasties.

Hours: M-F 11-9; Sa 11-7.
Cards: None.

## ENGLISH TEA SHOP {England} (n/r)

511 Irving St. San Francisco 564-2255

Not much British about its atmosphere; but this is probably the best place in the Bay Area to satisfy a crumpet craving. Try one with lemon curd or maple syrup ($1.00). Also available: *clotted cream*.

Hours: Tu-Sa 10-4.
Cards: No.

## PRINCE OF WALES {England} (n/r)

106 E. 25th. Ave. San Mateo 564-9723

A few British items like fish and chips at this English Pub, but many American accommodations. Versatile owner Jack Curry was once United States dart champion as well as fourth in the world in a chili cook off.

Hours: M-F 11(a)-12:00(m); Sa 12(n)-12(m).
Cards: None.

## HOUSE OF PRIME RIB {England} (n/r)

1906 Van Ness Ave. San Francisco 885-4605

A typical meat and potatoes joint masquerading as a purveyor of fine English cuisine but, oh what a beautiful rib!

Hours: M-Sa 5-11; Su 4-10.
Cards: V/MC.

## PENNY FARTHING {England} (n/r)

496 Hamilton Ave. Palo Alto 325-1994

Although billed as "English", the closest thing to a British item on Penny Farthing's menu is an English muffin.

Hours: M-Fr 7-3.
Cards: None. Checks accepted.

# CENTRAL
# NORTHERN
# EUROPE

## 2. CENTRAL AND NORTHERN EUROPE

*Denmark • Germany • The Netherlands • Sweden • Switzerland*

A short ferry ride is all that separates the British Isles from Holland and the beginning of our gastronomic journey to the nations of Northern and Central Europe. North-Central European cookery is dominated, as the region is geopolitically, by Germany. While nations such as the Netherlands and Denmark, Sweden and Switzerland all boast a number of interesting indigenous dishes, when one thinks of the cuisine of this region, one's thoughts inevitably turn to such items as *wiener schnitzel*, *wurst* and *strudel*--all Germanic innovations. For this reason--and because there are far more restaurants from Germany in the Bay Area than from anywhere else in North-Central Europe--in this introduction we will concentrate on the cuisine of Germany. The foods of other North-Central European lands will be discussed in the reviews of the restaurants which represent those countries.

### *Vorspeisen* (Appetizers)

While German restaurants tend to be big on *hauptgerichte* (entrees), they are relatively short on *vorspeisen*. In fact, many German restaurants offer no appetizers at all. When served, these are likely to include such items as *schwärzwalde schinken*--black forest ham, and *hering*--herring, usually either pickled or in a rich sour cream base. Suppen (soups) are also not the focal point of the German meal and salads, when offered, are often mixed with mayonnaise and potatoes and served as side dishes.

### *Hauptgerichte* (Entrées)

Germany is often thought of as a *meat and potatoes* sort of place, and with good reason; virtually every familiar German main course is likely to feature some sort of meat along with some sort of potatoes. Most Americans are familiar with at least a few common German entrees such as *wiener schnitzel*--delicately breaded milk-fed veal, and *sauerbraten*--tender sliced beef roasted in a marinade; as well as its wide variety of *wursts* (sausages), particularly *knackwurst*, *bratwurst* (veal) and *liverwurst*.

But there are other dishes that are common in Germany that are not so well known here. These include *rouladen*--a tender beefroll normally stuffed with onions and bacon, *kassler ripchen*--smoked pork loin, *rahmschnitzel*--veal with mushrooms in a wine cream sauce, *jäegerschnitzel*--medallions of pork in a red sauce, and *schweinshaxe*--slowly cooked pigs knuckles.

Most German entrees are accompanied by one or more side dishes which can be exceptional--sometimes the very best part of the meal. Common among these are *rotkohl*--pickled red cabbage, and *spätzle*--a small, tasty pasta sometimes substituted for *kartoffelsalat* (rich homemade German potato salad). In addition, some German restaurants offer cold meat and cheese plates. Finally *goulash*, although a Hungarian innovation, is an extremely popular dish in Germany and is often served at Germanic restaurants here.

## Getränke (Beverages) and Nachtisch (Desserts)

As everyone knows, Germans love to drink beer, and most German restaurants serve an extensive assortment of dark and light beers, often in huge steins. In addition, some German places will offer *glühwein*--a hot, spicy mulled wine, as well as liebfraumilch and other Rhine Wines. As far as desserts are concerned, we don't think we'd be letting the cat out if the bag by revealing that most German desserts, like most German entrees, are a tad on the heavy side. After all, Germany is the home of *käsetorte*--cheesecake, and *schwärzwalder kirschtorte*--black forest cherry cake, as well as the queen of all German desserts--*strudel*.

## SPECKMANN'S {Germany} (9/9=18)

1550 Church St.   San Francisco   282-6850

Speckmann's--a wonderful, intimate new world re-creation of a traditional Bavarian *bier-stube*--seems out of place in Noe Valley. But its bright, cheery atmosphere and perpetual "Oktoberfest" music makes memories of the "J" line fade and pictures of Switzerland and Southern Germany come alive. In addition to offering a ponderous choice of German beers, Speckmann's features a tempting array of *wursts* ($5.95--$6.95) and cold meat platters served on wooden trays. It also serves up the usual complement of traditional hot specialties like rouladen ($10.75), *jägerschnitzel* ($11.50) and *eisbein*--pig's knuckles ($11.50), and a hard to resist tray of traditional German strudels and torts. If your meal doesn't completely satisfy your craving for German food, you can proceed to Speckmann's adjacent deli, which stocks just about everything you might have a yen for from the old country, from apfelbutter to zwiebacks.

Hours: M-F 11-2, 5-9; Sa 11-10; Su 12-9.
Cards: All major.

## HOCHBURG VON GERMANIA {Germany} (8/9=17)

261 N. Second St.   San Jose   (408) 295-4484

Swords, helmets and medieval weapons are proudly displayed at this dark but lively restaurant-bar just off the main drag in downtown San Jose. If you are in the mood to make love and not war, you might want to pay a visit to Hochburg's cavernous formal ballroom, where dancing is open to the public on a weekly basis. If some good food is what you're after, you'll be pleased by Hochburg's thoroughly authentic menu which features the usual gamut of German specialty dishes--e.g. *sauerbraten* ($13.90) and *kassler ripchen* ($13.50)--as well as some other German dishes you're not quite as apt to be familiar with like *kalbshaxe*--a slow cooked shank of veal ($19.70 per person, for two). Hochburg's also offers an attractively priced selection of lunch specials ($5.50--$6.35). Finally, if desserts are you're thing, you'll surely enjoy Hochburg's real German *käsetorte* (cheesecake--$2.75). Danish sodas--somewhat more delicate than their American cousins--are also available ($1.35).

Hours: Daily 5-9:30; M-F 11:30--2.
Cards: MC/V.

## GERMAN COOK {Germany} (8/7=15)

612 O'Farrell St.   San Francisco   776-9022

   Hand-painted wooden chairs, beer steins and a wall length mural of a pastoral Central European scene greet you as you walk through the doors of the German Cook. This restaurant, which has been in continuous operation for more than a quarter century, now seems somewhat out of place amongst the crowd of mostly Southeast Asian restaurants and bars which have recently sprung up in the area. Further, the German Cook's menu is not elaborate, and there is nothing that you will see here that you would not be able to obtain at other local German restaurants. The German Cook is, however, still quite pleasant. It serves good, hearty German food at some of the best prices in town; and boasts a gregarious, authentic Central European atmosphere. The old standbys--*sauerbraten*, *wiener schnitzel* and *bratwurst* (veal sausage)--are all tasty and cheap, with nothing over $8.00; and the German Cook's side dishes, especially its boiled potatoes and *rotkohl*, are among the best around.

Hours: Daily 4:30-10.
Cards: All Major.

## SCHROEDER'S CAFE {Bavaria} (8/6=14)

240 Front St.   San Francisco   421-4778

   Schroeder's--a fairly authentic replica of an old Bavarian beer hall--is dominated by a massive amount of mahogany, polished oak tables, and a series of huge murals painted by Herman Richter in 1932. It also boasts a large number of beer steins, including a large phallic-looking one near the door, nice stained glass, and appropriately gussied up waiters in black tie. Seating is "traditional style"--which means you will often find yourself sitting with someone you don't know. Even before you sit down rye bread, homemade potato salad and excellent cole slaw are waiting. The menu is on the board, with some items changing daily and others staying the same. Most notable among Schroeder's regular German features are *sauerbraten and red cabbage* ($8.95) and a *German sausage platter*. Even these dishes are unspectacular however, and if you don't order a soup or dessert, will leave you hungry. Although Schroeder's showcases Bavarian, not German cuisine, you're not apt to notice any difference.

Hours: M-F 11-9.
Cards: AE/MC/V.

## TESKE'S {Germany} (7/7=14)

255 N. First St.   San Jose   (408) 292-0291

This venerable San Jose establishment--with its animal heads and other Teutonic ornaments--is attractive but perhaps too capacious for its own good. The sheer volume of its two dark wood dining rooms negates the possibility of an intimate dining experience. These give way to an equally imposing outdoor beer garden, replete with a lion's head fountain and fragrant flowers. Reasonable lunch specials ($5.75-$8.75) include *spiess braten*--stuffed curry roast pork with hot potato salad ($7.75).

Hours: Tu-F--11-2, 5--9:30; Sa--5-9:30.
Cards: MC/V.

## OLD SWISS HOUSE {Switzerland} (7/6=13)

Pier 39   San Francisco   434-0432

Bells on belts, extensive interior woodwork, lace curtains, beautiful brightly-colored china from Luxembourg, a couple of lovely clocks and carved-heart chairs make the Old Swiss House a place to visit even though it offers only a few Swiss dishes such as *spaghetti Ticinese*--with ham and tomatoes ($6.75), seems kind of cold, is hard to park near (cheaply, at least), and suffers from an overabundance of tourists.

Hours: Daily 11:30-4, 5-10.
Cards: All major.

## MATTERHORN {Switzerland} (6/7=13)

2323 Van Ness Ave.   San Francisco   885-6116

An inviting menu at this genuine but somewhat pricy Swiss miss. How authentic is the Matterhorn? Its interior was actually made in Switzerland, shipped over, and assembled here. You'll find all the old Swiss favorites on its menu including *rahschnitzel*--veal ($17.00), *fondue* and *raclette*--an appetizer made from an indigenous type of Swiss cheese ($6.00). For dessert, how about chocolate fondue ($5.00)?

Hours: 5:30-10.
Cards: V/MC.

## NORDIC GOURMET KAFE {Denmark} (n/r)

444 Jackson St.  Hayward  886-0651

A quaint and pretty place which, with its pointy A-frame roof, looks something like a Scandinavian diner. A large cuckoo clock, lace curtains and other North European touches help the atmosphere; and the somewhat authentic menu features *gravalax* (smoked salmon), *Danish red cabbage* and other Scandinavian specialties. Last time we visited, however, the Kafe was closed at a time when it should have been open "until further notice". So we'll reserve further comment to the next edition of this book.

Hours: T-F 11-9, Sa-Su 8(a)-9(p) but see above.
Cards: V/MC.

## COPENHAGEN {Denmark} (n/r)

1216 Burlingame Ave.  Burlingame  342-1357

Not much about the Copenhagen is calculated to make you feel like you are actually in Denmark. However, it is nice to sit near the window and watch all the people strolling along Burlingame Avenue. Some of Copenhagen's more authentic Northern European offerings are *Danish liverpaste* and Danish apple pie. Fawlty Towers fans will want to try Copenhagen's *waldorf salad* ($5.25).

Hours: Daily 6-6 (except Su 8-4).
Cards: None. Checks accepted.

## GERMAN OAK {Bavaria} (n/r)

2257 Market St.  San Francisco  861-9669

This is an aesthetically-pleasing place, with chorale music and oak-panelled walls, and it offers many reasonably priced German specials such as *bratwurst* ($6.75), *paprika schnitzel* ($9.65) and *kassler ripchen*--smoked pork loin ($8.60). Still, there are many better German places around.

Hours: Tu-Su 5-9:45; Sa 5-10:45.
Cards: V/MC.

## ANDRE'S CONFISERIE SUISSE {Switzerland} (n/r)

898 Santa Cruz Ave.   Menlo Park   325-4776

With its primary emphasis on baked goods, this doesn't quite qualify as an authentic Swiss dining experience. It does, however, boast inviting Swiss travel posters and those cute little chairs with the hearts cut out.

Hours: Tu-F 9-5:30; F-Sa 9-9.
Cards: No.

## DE WINDMOLEN {The Netherlands} (n/r)

1220 Ninth Ave.   San Francisco   753-0557

Everything at De Windmolen is informal (they answer the phone "hello") and you get decent food for the price, but you won't find yourself phoning KLM after a visit there.

Hours: Every day 8(a)-9(p).
Cards: AE.

## SWEDEN HOUSE {Sweden} (n/r)

35 Main St.   Tiburon   435-9767

Nothing to write home to Goteborg about except an idyllic harbor view. Enjoy a pastry outside with the sea gulls, but don't expect Bjorn Borg to stroll in.

Hours: M-F 8-5; Sa-Su 8:30-7.
Cards: No. Personal checks accepted.

## BLACK FOREST INN {Germany} (n/r)

376 First St.   Los Altos   948-5031

A somewhat authentic German restaurant with decent food and mediocre service in a pleasant, scenic location.

Hours: Tu-Th 11:30-8:30, F-Sa 11-9.
Cards: AE/MC/V.

## LIPPIZANER {Austria} (n/r)

1242 Fourth St.  San Rafael  459-2202

Nominally "Viennese", but Lippizaner's cuisine is more French. It is also ultramodern, with little to distinguish its decor. Lippizaner does offer an elaborate Sunday brunch, however ($17.50).

Hours: M-Sa 11-3, 5-10; Su 10-3.
Cards: MC/V.

## FONDUE FRED'S {Switzerland} (n/r)

2556 Telegraph Ave.  Berkeley  549-0850

The name gives this one away. Plenty of fondue, but hold the Swiss.

Hours: Tu-F 12(n)-10; Sa-Su 12(n)-12(m).
Cards: MC/V/AE.

# SOUTHERN EUROPE

# 3. SOUTHERN EUROPE

*The Basque Region • Greece • Portugal • Spain*

In addition to Italian which, because it is so familiar to most Americans, is not included in this book, there are 3 other "major" Southern European cultures--Spanish, Portuguese and Greek--and one "minor" one--Basque. Each of these cultures, their national cuisines and representative restaurants will be discussed in this chapter. For ease of reference, the chapter is divided into two general categories: *Iberia*--which encompasses Spain, Portugal and the Basque Region--and *Greece*.

## Iberia

*The Basque Region • Portugal • Spain*

### Tapas (*Apertivos*--Appetizers)

Although Iberian appetizers vary greatly, you are liable to be offered some form of *almejas* (*ameijoas*)--clams, usually in *ajo* (garlic) and/or *chorizo* (*linguica*)--sausage, possibly in a *jerez* (sherry) sauce. People throughout Iberia also tend to relish thick, rich soups such as *sopa de mariscos*--seafood soup, and *gazpacho*--the traditional cold vegetable soup from the Spanish province of Andalusia.

### *Entradas* (Entrées) and *Postres* (Desserts)

While Iberia boasts splendid recipes for all kinds of *aves*--poultry, and *carnes*--meats; its proximity to the sea leads to a natural emphasis on *mariscos*--shellfish and *pescados* (*peixes*)--fish. Some popular aquatic Spanish favorites are *pargo*--red snapper, sometimes eaten *a la molinera* (in a lemon, butter sauce); *calamares a la malaguena*--deep fried baby squid; *zarzuela*--shellfish and fish sauted in white wine, brandy, garlic and tomato sauce; *gambas al ajillo*--jumbo prawns grilled in garlic; and, of course, *paella marinera*--a glorious seafood casserole filled with lobster, clams, mussels and a huge portion of aromatic Spanish *zafron* "saffron" rice. Portugal borrows heavily from this list, then adds a couple of splendid fish and seafood dishes of its own, most notably *bacalhau*--

codfish, often eaten *a Gomes de Sa*--baked in olive oil; and *polvo*--octopus, generally enjoyed *guisado* (in a white wine sauce).

Popular Spanish meat dishes include *estofado de res*--beef stew with red wine, vegetables and spices; *arroz con pollo*--chicken with rice; *pollo al jerez*--chicken sauted in sherry; *lomo de cerdo*--sauteed pork loin; and *paella Valenciana*--a mixed meat and seafood combination which adds such items as chicken and sausage to the recipe for *paella marinera*. Possibly the definitive Portuguese meat offering is *bife a Portuguesa*--an interesting combination of grilled steak and eggs. However, Portugal also offers its own version of Polish *bigos* and German *jagerschnitzel*. Called *coelho a cacadora*, this traditional Portuguese *hunter's stew* features braised rabbit in a rich sauce.

Although perhaps more familiar to Bay Area residents as Latin American hand-me-downs, many good desserts got their start in Iberia. Most familiar of these are *flan con crema* (*pudim flan*)--caramel custard, and *arroz con leche*--rice pudding.

### Basque Cuisine

The Basque Region straddles the border between France and Spain. While a few local Basque establishments emphasize "Spanish Basque" cuisine, the majority specialize in the cuisine of the Basque section of France. Two dishes, however, tend to show up on all Basque menus--*oxtail stew* and *sweetbreads; the latter being* brains, usually of veal. Although neither dish is familiar to most Americans, in the Basque Region they are considered great delicacies.

Whether "French Basque" or "Spanish Basque", local representatives of the Basque Region tend to serve meals "family style". This means that they are multi-course affairs with bountiful tureens of soup, huge salads and the like, in which everyone shares. But it also means that, with the possible exception of entrees, there is very little choice afforded and, as you would at home, you must take what you are given and enjoy it.

## EL OSO {Spain} (9/10=19)

1153 Valencia St.   San Francisco   550-0601

El Oso is attractively appointed and highly ornate. While a bit more gauche (we could do without all the bearskins and the gun collection) than our former favorite, the now defunct "El Meson", El Oso does boast museum-quality paintings, some of the nicest stained glass you'll ever see in a restaurant, and many wonderful small touches including a genuine marble fireplace displaying a lovely vase and clock. You'll find that there is much animated conversation and laughter at El Oso, even in the middle of a weekday afternoon. Still, all of El Oso's beauty and good cheer would mean little if its food were forgettable. If anything, however, El Oso's food is better than its ambience. Certainly it serves the best *gazpacho* in the Bay Area and, with the possible exception of Alejandro's, offers more and better Spanish *tapas* then anywhere else around (try its *Galician-style octopus*--$6.50). El Oso's fine collection of a la carte entrees include such unusual dishes as *codornizes estofados*--cognac and wine over oven baked quail, as well as more familiar ones like *cazuela de mariscos variedades*--mixed shellfish ($14.40); and, of course, *paella marinera* ($30.00 for two). If you are only in the mood for a light bite, you might consider sampling a *boccadillo*--a popular Spanish sandwich made from grilled meats such as *lomo adobado*--pork loin, and *ternera*--veal; or a *tortilla* (different from the Mexican kind--these are Spanish-style omelettes), especially the one made with *chorizo* (Spanish sausage). They are out of this world. If you look on the back of what might well be the city's most colorful menu, you will note that El Oso also offers a wide variety of daily lunch specials for under $10.00. Also, don't plan on leaving until you've tried one of its exquisite desserts, the best of which may be *natillas castellanas*--a soft, light custard ($1.25). Throughout your meal, live piano music is played and the service at El Oso, if not perfect (our cold soup and hot entree arrived at the same time), is at least genial and enthusiastic. Possibly the worst thing about the restaurant is that a few Mexican specials are offered but, otherwise, both menu and ambience reflect a loyalty to the mother country that epitomizes what we like most about ethnic restaurants. Indeed, places like El Oso, easily the finest restaurant of any kind in or anywhere near the Mission District, make you wonder why people ever bother to go anywhere else.

Hours: Every day 11-3; 6-11.
Cards: All major.

## BASQUE CULTURAL CENTER {Basque} (8/10=18)

599 Railroad Ave.  South San Francisco  583-8091

Maybe it's just because this is far and away the best restaurant of any kind for miles around but--despite its "dare you to find me" location--the Basque Cultural Center packs them in. They're not here for the uniquely shaped structure that houses not only the restaurant, but a rare three-walled jai alai court, or any of the numerous other cultural activities carried on by the center's over 400 members. They are also not here for the Center's fine display of Basque indigenous items like "galtza motxa"--wool leg warmers and "sheepherder's bread". No, what they are after is unparalleled French Basque cuisine--especially the Center's traditional Basque "family-style" dinners ($10.00--$12.00). You may think you are imagining that the restaurant's soup and salad are among the best you've ever tasted, but try a seafood or chicken crepe and you'll be convinced. And, oh that Basque cake!

Hours: Tu-F 11:30--2:30; Tu-Sa 5:30-9:30; Su 5-9.
Cards: V/MC.

## EL PATIO {Spain} (9/9=18)

2850 Alemany Blvd.  San Francisco  587-5117

Not to be outdone by their ethnic neighbors to the north, the Spanish have established their own attractive cultural center which--like its Basque counterpart--boasts a wonderful restaurant, El Patio, with a light, airy atmosphere, black wrought iron, skylights, lots of plants and marvellous service. El Patio features family-style renditions of Spain's finest regional cuisine. Of El Patios's many specials, which change daily, some of the most interesting are *pollo chilindron*--chicken sauteed with pimientos and ham in a white wine sauce ($11.25); *estofado de res*--the traditional Spanish beef stew with carrots, spices and red wine; and *canilla de cordero*--lamb shanks braised in a brandy and beer sauce ($12.50). El Patio's lunch *specials*, which start at about $7.00, include such traditional Spanish favorites as *pargo a la molinera, lomo de cerdo* and (Spanish-style) *tortillas*. But don't miss the *paella* here ($28.00 for two).

Hours: M, W-F 11:30-2:30; W-M 5:30-9:30. Su Brunch 12-3.
Cards: All major.

## TAMAR {Portugal} (9/7=16)

1612 Alum Rock Ave.   San Jose   (408) 258-5656

Tamar, our favorite of the small cluster of Portuguese places which line a two block stretch of Santa Clara and Alum Rock Avenues in San Jose, has a storefront so small you could easily walk right by. But the restaurant is deep--not only in area but in Portuguese charm. We hesitate to describe Tamar's decor because proprietor Jorge Sousa (no relation to the Sousas of "Sousa's", next door) recently returned from Portugal with all new *objets d'art* for his store. Presumably Tamar's lovely Portuguese ceramics and inviting pictures of the Azores will survive renovation. Certainly the restaurant's most memorable fixtures--its gorgeous Iberian tiles--will still be there; as will its relaxing patio garden (which, unfortunately, has been partially obliterated by a satellite dish). Nor, Sousa assured us, will the restaurant's authentic menu--which features such typical Iberian dishes as *mariscada* ($14.95), and *bacalhau a bras* (shredded codfish with potatoes-$7.75)--undergo radical change.

Hours: Daily 11-9.
Cards: No. Personal checks accepted.

## SILVA'S {Portugal} (7/8=15)

1527 E. Santa Clara   San Jose   (408) 729-4011

Silva's, the newest member of San Jose's Portuguese restaurant fraternity, is not particularly fancy and does not possess all the Portuguese paraphernalia you find at places like Tamar and Sousa's right down the street. But a place that is always abuzz with animated conversation in the mother tongue can't be all bad, and Silva's food is right out of Oporto. As with most Portuguese places, Silva's best dishes are its various seafood combinations. However, if it's a specialty dish like *mariscada* that you want, you must order ahead or be prepared to wait an hour or more. If you can't wait, try Silva's traditional fried cod with potatoes and vegetables ($6.50), or one of its wide selection of meat dishes. We particularly enjoy Silva's fresh homemade bread and, at a dollar a glass, it's hard not to like its seemingly freshly-stamped house wine too. Finally, Silva's offers some tempting desserts. Try the *"lemon mousse"*. *It's* really just lemon meringue pie, but it's still very good ($1.50).

Hours: Daily: 7(a)-9(p).
Cards: No.

## BANDIDOS OF THE SEA {Spain} (9/5=14)

31014 Union City Blvd.   Union City   489-7999

With a tile and stained glass bar, an entire wall devoted to bullfight posters, Spanish bagpipes, black wrought iron wine racks, and one of the largest hand-painted murals you're ever likely to see on a restaurant wall (about 25 feet), Bandidos is easily one of the most interesting of all Bay Area ethnic restaurants. But its stunning Mediterranean design seems painfully out of place in, and is wasted on, this poorly travelled section of Union City. Add to this an outside patio which seems as though it hasn't been in use since the Spanish Civil War, and you have ample reason to wonder how a restaurant with so much going for it could go so far wrong. Similarly, Bandidos' exquisite colonial Spanish decor stands in rude contrast to its mediocre fare, only some of which is nominally Spanish. Particularly questionable is its "fishy" *paella marinera* ($25.00 for two). With better food and a more accessible location, this could be a top ten restaurant.

Hours: M-F 11-3; Daily 5-10.
Cards: All major.

## EL GALLEGO {Spain} (5/6=11)

3161 24th St.   San Francisco   821-6300

Anyone who thinks the business of writing restaurant reviews is uncomplicated should have been with us when we first visited El Gallego. The restaurant had been advertised as being "Spanish and Italian"; but, upon our arrival, we learned it was now claiming to be Spanish and *Mexican*. If this weren't disconcerting enough, the menu opened to reveal offerings from neither Spain, Italy or Mexico--such as Filipino *lumpias*. Then the time came to subjectively assess the restaurant's decor--the primary components of which were a series of Picasso-esque water colors. This done, we were relaxing over a cup of coffee, putting the finishing touches on our review, when two men in a van arrived. Within minutes they had carefully and meticulously boxed up and carted out all of the paintings. Recently we were informed that El Gallego's menu had changed again, but when we called to find out, its telephone had been disconnected. Stay tuned.

Hours: Tu-Su 11-9, but see above.
Cards: All major.

## SOUSA'S {Portugal} (4/7=11)

1614 Alum Rock Ave.  San Jose  (408) 926-9075

Plenty of lovely paintings and beautiful tiles, but Sousa's, which used to be among our favorites, is living proof of how begrudging service can ruin otherwise pleasant atmosphere. Try *polvo*--octopus stew ($9.75).

Hours: Daily 6-11.
Cards: All major.

## CHALET BASQUE {Basque} (5/5=10)

405 N. San Pedro Ave.  San Rafael

Chalet Basque has decent atmosphere and offers nicely presented family-style dinners at a reasonable price, but its ambience is not particularly authentic, and its food is only fair.

Hours: Tu-F 11:30-2, 5-10; Sa 5-10, Su (brunch) 10:30-2;, 4-9.
Cards: MC/V.

## IBERIA {Spain} (4/6=10)

190 Ladera Country Shopper  Portola Valley  854-1746

Quite pricy (average price for entrees--$14.00) and not particularly Spanish-looking, but Iberia does have a following (dinner reservations are recommended), and its food is quite good.

Hours: 11:30-2:30, 5:30-10.
Cards: All major.

## ALEJANDRO'S {Spain} (n/r)

1840 Clement St.  San Francisco  668-1184

Although Spanish tapas and entrees are served, Alejandro's emphasis is on Peruvian cuisine. We discuss it in more detail in Chapter 10.

Hours: M-Th 5-11; F-Sa 5-12; Su 4-11.
Cards: All major.

## PATUSCO'S {Portugal} (n/r)

300 Park Ave.  Alameda  523-2525

Although ostensibly "Portuguese-American", there is little to peg this pleasant brick and glass place as Portuguese. Nevertheless, reservations are recommended on Friday and Saturday nights.

Hours: M-F 11-9:30; Sa-Su 8(a)-9:30(p).
Cards: All major. No checks.

## CABRILLO RESTAURANT {Portugal} (n/r)

57 Washington St.  Santa Clara  (408) 248-2575

Capacious dining room offers only the faintest hint of the Cabrillo's Portuguese heritage, and no sign makes it hard to find. Recent telephone disconnect could signal curtains.

Hours: M-Sa 11:30--7, but see above.
Cards: All major.

## DES ALPES {BASQUE} (n/r)

732 Broadway  San Francisco  391-4249

Decent Basque family style dinners in a typical, but not particularly memorable environment.

Hours: Tu-Sa 5:30-10. Su 5-9:30.
Cards: V/MC.

# GREECE

There are, of course, beautiful places all over the world. We love Afghanistan, for example, in an almost mystical sense, and for intrigue and some types of shopping there is no place like Istanbul's Grand Bazaar. But overall, if we had to pick one part of the world to go back to, again and again, it would be Greece. At once placid and vital, miraculous but still brutally human, Greece enchants you with glorious islands, tranquil Mediterranean waters, and the *joie de vivre* of the Greek people themselves.

Then, too, there is the food. Few countries so small have made as profound an impression on the international palate as Greece. Certainly, in not many ethnic restaurants are you more apt to have a memorable experience than in one that mirrors the Greek lust for life. You don't have to visit many such restaurants before you realize that regular visits to them will warm your soul as well as satisfy your craving for extraordinary food.

## *Mezethakia* (Appetizers)

For our drachmas, the Greeks have conceived more and better mezethakia (appetizers) than just about anybody else in the world. Most Americans are familiar with at least two of these, *spanakopitas*--spinach pies, and *tiropitas*--cheese pies, both baked in *filo* (phylo) dough. But other wonderful Greek appetizers--such as *taramosalata*, *tzatziki* and *dolmades*--are less well known.

"Taramo" is a filling and satisfying red caviar dip which is spread on Greek bread. When homemade, "taramo" is slightly coarse and gritty, but has a wonderful, tangy taste. *Tzatziki*--the Mediterranean equivalent of Indian *raita* and Persian *mast-o-khiar*--is a delightful combination of yogurt, cucumbers and dill. It too is tangy when fresh. *Dolmades*, an acquired taste because of their slightly acrid tang, are grape leaves stuffed with meat. These are enjoyed throughout the Middle East and North Africa, as well as in Greece.

Other common Greek appetizers are *locanico*--a spicy sausage sometimes flavored with orange; *saganiki*--made from Greek *kasseri* cheese dipped in bread crumbs and eggs, then sauteed; and *keftethes*--small Greek meatballs. Greece is also justifiably famous for its superb Greek salads, particularly *maroulosalata*--lettuce, onions, feta cheese and tangy kalamata olives, and *horiatikisalata*--the same basic ingredients with more fresh tomatoes; as well as *avgolemono*--literally *egg/lemon* soup.

### Entrées

Many Americans, particularly on the East Coast, are well acquainted with certain Greek short order items such as *souvlakia*--skewers of charbroiled meat, and *gyros*--fresh sliced roast lamb sandwiches (the Greek equivalent of Middle Eastern *shwarmas*). In New York and other East Coast cities, these are sold by street vendors the same way that hot dogs are. Few of us, however, especially in California, are familiar with the gamut of more sophisticated entrees routinely enjoyed in Greece.

To truly know Greek food there are dozens of entrees you would want to try, but there are certain items which appear with regularity on local Greek menus. Some of our favorites are *arni pisto*--roast leg of lamb with garlic and lemon; *brizoles*--marinated lamb chops; *moussaka*--sauteed eggplant layered with ground beef and baked in bechamel sauce; *pasticio*--pasta with meat and tomatoes, sometimes referred to as "Greek lasagna"; *psari plaki*--filet of rock cod baked in a light tomato sauce; *kalamarakia*--fried or sauteed squid; and *koto lemono*--chicken with lemon. Not quite as common here, but certainly just as good, are *koto kapama*--sauteed chicken and vegetables in wine sauce; *exohiko*--lamb with sauteed vegetables and kasseri cheese wrapped in filo; *skorpios*--sauteed prawns in a wine, feta and garlic sauce; and *goulbasi*--slow cooked lamb on the shank with garlic and cheese.

### Desserts and Beverages

Although Greece boasts an astonishing variety of desserts, few local Greek establishments carry anything close to a full range of them. The one you will most often see is *baklava*--a sweet honeyed pastry much beloved throughout the Middle East and even in India. Two others you will likely come across, and should definitely try, are *rizogalo*--rice pudding, and *galatobouriko*--custard topped with filo. Some restaurants also serve Greek (sometimes referred to as "Turkish" or "Arabic") coffee. This is a highly concentrated blend which is slowly brewed with sugar. Although usually drunk by the Greeks "medium sweet", it can be made as sweet as you like.

Finally, though they may not appear on the menu, most Greek restaurants stock an ample supply of Greek wines. Over the years we have come to believe that no Greek meal is complete without a glass of *retsina*--a pungent Greek "resin" wine made from pine needles. Few people like retsina the first time around. However, you can get used to it pretty quickly, especially in Greece, where large bottles sell for less than two dollars apiece.

## ATHENS BY NIGHT {Greece} (9/8=17)

811 Valencia St.  San Francisco  647-3744

The atmosphere of Athens by Night is among the most unusual around. An engaging Greek restaurant-bar, it might better be called "Caverns by Night" because of the amazing job done to make its bar look and feel like a genuine Greek grotto. Water actually runs down the side of its wall while live birds in cages merrily chirp away. Also, with the possible exception of El Oso, right down the street, there may be no bar in the Bay Area which displays more figurines and other gewgaws than the one at Athens. Athens' restaurant part is more formal, with fresh flowers, tablecloths, somber portraits and the like. It is there you will enjoy wonderfully authentic Greek specials like *exohiko*--lamb with sauteed vegetables and kasseri cheese wrapped in filo dough ($13.95), and *chicken kapama*--sauteed in wine sauce with Greek spices ($8.95). Athens By Night may be a tad overpriced, but its atmosphere warrants the expense.

Hours: Daily 11(a)-2(a).
Cards: MC/V.

## ATHENS GREEK RESTAURANT {Greece} (8/8=16)

39 Mason St.  San Francisco  775-1929

As all travellers know, the key to great adventure is serendipity--the gift of looking for one thing and finding something else. We headed to the "Tenderloin" one day looking for the Greek Village, a trendy establishment in what used to be San Francisco's small Greek town. The Village was closed, but we happened to spot a small sign indicating that Athens Greek Restaurant was ready and waiting. This intimate Taverna offers food and service so authentic you'll feel like your having dinner at a Greek friend's home. Also, for a place the size of our kitchen, it serves an enormous variety of reasonably priced dishes, such as a heaping plate of *moussaka* for only $5.75. You might try any of Athens' stuffed dishes--eggplant, peppers or dolmas ($4.75) or seven lamb dishes (none over $7.00); and a glass of retsina big enough to chase away the Tenderloin blues sells for less than a buck. Athens may not be chic or beautiful, but few ethnic restaurants better personify the feeling of their native land.

Hours: M-Sa 11-10.
Cards: None.

## MORNING STAR {Greece} (8/6=14)

3814 Piedmont Ave.   Oakland   658-3311

The interior alcoves of the Morning Star vibrate with cheerful bouzouki music. Look around and you will see a collection of Greek mementos, including island posters and pictures. Outside, a tranquil patio comes alive with trellises, hanging vines and traditional blue-checkered tablecloths. While the restaurant's limited number of Greek entrees are, by in large, just a bit above average, the Morning Star does offer some superb Greek appetizers, particularly homemade *taramosalata* ($3.95) and *tzatziki*.

Hours: Su-Th 10-3, 5-9; F-Sa 10-3, 5-10.
Cards: All Major.

## S. ASIMAKOPOULOS CAFE {Greece} (4/7=11)

288 Connecticut St.   San Francisco   552-8789

It has a Greek name and sports the Greek colors (blue and white), but somehow this trendy Portrero Hill establishment doesn't quite capture the Greek spirit. Among the high points: fresh flowers and whirling ceiling fans reminiscent of the Greek Islands. Among the low points: a cramped interior, few Greek *objets d'art* and an overpriced menu. Plus, where's the music? Best bet: *galatobouriko*--milk pudding.

Hours: M-F 11:30-10; Sa-Su 5-10.
Cards: MC/V/AE.

## SALONIKA {Greece} (5/6=11)

2237 Polk St.   San Francisco   771-2077

Somewhat pretty but too formal (one might almost say sterile) for our tastes. Inviting bouzouki music, wrought iron over red brick arches, and some nice little red-framed pictures of typical Greek scenes help smooth some of Salonika's rough edges. However Salonika's Greek offerings, though abundant, are a bit costly. For example, the restaurant's four *pikilia* (small portions of a host of Greek dishes) run $14.00--$18.50.

Hours: Tu-Sa 5:30-11; Su 5-10.
Cards: MC/V.

## PANOS {Greece} (n/r)

4000 24th St. San Francisco   824-8000

Panos' blah, modern atmosphere is only partially redeemed by its wonderful *galatobouriko*. The restaurant serves a wide range of Greek appetizers; otherwise, its menu is too eclectic to be authentic.

Hours: Daily 5-10; Sa-Su 10-2:30.
Cards: MC/V.

## STOYANOF'S {Greece} (n/r)

1240 Ninth Ave. San Francisco   664-3664

Few Greek touches at what is, at root, a soup and (feta) salad place. However, if you've never had a *borek* (stuffed filo dough), this is a good place to try one ($1.50). Stoyanof's serves many Greek specials nightly.

Hours: Tu-Su 10-9:30 (F-Sa until 10).
Cards: Only accepted at dinner--MC/V/AE.

## VERONA {Greece} (n/r)

291 30th St. San Francisco   821-6900

Verona surprises with a variety of interesting Greek specialties, including *arni psito* and roast lamb leg with garlic ($11.00). Unfortunately, its atmosphere is more Italian than Greek, and not very much of either.

Hours: Daily 11:30-11.
Cards: All major.

## THE ACORN {Greece} (n/r)

1906 El Camino Real   Menlo Park   322-6201

While nominally "Mediterranean", with a few nice Greek dishes like *skorpios*, the Acorn has no Greek atmosphere, and is on the costly side.

Hours: M-F 11:30-2; 5-11; Sa-Su 5-10.
Cards: All major.

## MIKE'S XLNT FOODS {Greece} (n/r)

905 S. Bascom Ave.  San Jose  (408) 294-2262

Mike (Thomas actually) places too much emphasis on pizza for our liking, but he also offers a variety of good Greek dishes, including moussaka, and the price is right.

Hours: M-Th 6(a)-9(p); F-Sa 6(a)--9:30; Su 7(a)-8:30.
Cards: All major. Personal checks accepted.

## MYKONOS RESTAURANT {Greece} (n/r)

2110 Shattuck Ave.  Berkeley  841-8766

There is some Greek ambience in this cafeteria-style delicatessen, but Mykonos looks considerably more authentic that it tastes.

Hours: M-F 8:30-7:30; Sa 8:30-6:30.
Cards: None.

# EASTERN EUROPE

## 4. EASTERN EUROPE

*Czechoslovakia • Hungary • Poland • Russia • Yugoslavia*

Once upon a time, many years ago, as many as a dozen establishments specializing in the joyous presentation of rich, Russian fare carried on a brisk business within the city limits of San Francisco alone. Sadly, those days are gone. A younger generation of Russian restaurants has, however, recently begun to take root in various spots around the bay. Further, Northern California's non-Russian Eastern European restaurant community, though small, can claim among its number several of the very best ethnic restaurants of any type in the Bay Area today.

The main influence on Eastern European cuisine, as on all things Eastern European, is Russia. However, a number of other East European nations--most notably Poland, Hungary and Czechoslovakia--have carved out their own distinctive brand of East European fare. Still, there are far more similarities than differences, both in atmosphere and cuisine, between most good Eastern European restaurants.

Since no one country presently dominates the Bay Area's East European restaurant scene, we will not discuss the various national cuisines of Eastern Europe separately. When discussing a particular dish or beverage, however, we will do our best to let you know which country it comes from. All foreign words used in this introduction will be in Russian unless otherwise indicated.

### *Zakuska* (Hors D'Oeuvres) and Soups

With the possible exception of France, no regional cuisine is richer in appetizers than is Eastern European cuisine; and when we say "rich", we mean *rich*, starting with *seledka* (Polish: *sledz*)--marinated herring, sometimes served in a thick sour cream sauce. Other traditional East European *zakuska*, traditionally downed with a large glass of cold vodka, are *pashtet* (Polish: *watrobka po polska;* Hungarian: *kacsamaj*)--chopped chicken liver pate; *sliwki* (Polish)--prunes rolled in hot bacon; *beluga ikra* --black caviar; *eggs a la Russe* with caviar; *blini*--sour dough yeast pancakes served with sour cream; *hotobagyi palascinta* (Hungarian)-- crepes stuffed with meat; and *kabanocy flambe* (Polish)--Polish sausages flamed in vodka.

The king of Eastern European soups is, of course, *borscht* (Polish: *barszcz*)--that odd blend of cabbage, beets and sour cream which may be served hot or cold, depending on the season. While homemade borscht can be delightful, our favorite Eastern European soup is *hideg megyleves*-- (Hungarian)--cold cherry soup. Other interesting regional soups are *pelmeni*--the Russian equivalent of ravioli in broth; *grochowka*--a Polish soup made with sweet peas and ham; and, last but not least, *gulyas* (goulash)--the classic Hungarian beef and potato stew which, when made in traditional fashion, is laced with a liberal dose of paprika, then cooked over an open fire in a thin-walled portable iron kettle called a *bogracs*.

### Entrées

Many Eastern European entrees have become so familiar to Americans that they may be offered, with little or no explanation, on American menus. In addition to borscht and goulash, there are a number of entrees which fit this description. Chief among these are *pierogi* (Polish)--shells of pasta filled with meat, cheese and mushrooms, then lightly fried in sour cream and butter; *blinchiki* (blintzes)--Russian crepes; *chicken Kiev*--a breast of chicken with minced mushrooms, sometimes served with bechamel sauce; and *beef stroganoff*--the classic Russian dish of beef flambeed in brandy, then sauteed in a rich mushroom cream sauce.

Less well known here are *golabki* (Polish; Ukranian: *golubtzy;* Hungarian: *toltott kaposzta*)--baked stuffed cabbage; *parikas csirke* (Hungarian)--chicken with paprika; *grape pula* (Czech)--grape leaves stuffed with chunks of pork in a paprika sauce; *vareniky*--thin dough stuffed with farmers cheese, served with sour cream; *sirniki* (Polish: sernik)--"pancakes" made from eggs, sugar and cottage cheese--sometimes eaten as a dessert; and *bigos*--a hunter's stew that was once a staple of the country estates of Polish nobles. While, in olden days, all kinds of wild game and venison may have been thrown into the *bigos* pot, nowadays the meat which gives bigos its distinctive flavor is almost certain to be rabbit. Bigos is still considered to be the Polish national dish.

## Desserts

Eastern Europe has also made more than a little mark on the world of desserts. In addition to *blinchiki* (blintzes) and *sirniki*, both of which may appear either as appetizers or--when served with strawberry sour cream or lemon cheese--as desserts; we owe thanks to Eastern Europe for such contributions as *palascinta*--Hungarian crepes; *palascinki*--Czechoslovakian crepe suzettes (usually served with either cottage cheese or apricot preserves); *plombir*--rich Russian fruit ice cream; and two Hungarian tortes, *sacher* (sweet chocolate) and *dobos*. *Dobos* torte is a delicate multi-layer cake with a brittle caramel crust--one of our all-time favorites.

## GYPSY CELLAR (THE) {Czechoslovakia} (10/10=20)
932 Middlefield Rd.   Redwood City   371-1166

Gypsies have a maligned reputation but, to the traveller, the word "gypsy" conjures up nothing but positive images. So, for that matter, does the word "cellar". Therefore, based on its name, one might think that the Gypsy Cellar would be quite a find. Of course, names can sometimes be deceiving and, from the outside of the building, which looks like it was once an International House of Pancakes, you can be forgiven for having your doubts. But it is what is inside that counts, and what is inside is a hands down top ten selection, easily one of the best East European restaurants in the western United States. Imagine: a plush, brightly-colored canopy overhangs authentic lanterns with dim lights, dolls in native costume, and traditional East European flower paintings on exposed wood beams. Now, blend in waitpeople dressed in colorful native attire, live Eastern European music--including a strolling violin serenade--and some superb Czech and Hungarian cuisine. It could be Budapest. It could be Prague. With wonderful East European dishes like *segedin goulash*--cubed pork sauteed in paprika sauce with sour cream ($13.95); *saslik Enesco*--grilled sirloin on a skewer with vegetables, bacon, mushrooms and rice pilaf ($15.95); *juliska paprikas*--chicken with a paprika and sour cream sauce ($12.95); and *grape pula*--grape leaves stuffed with ground beef and rice with sour cream ($10.95); the Gypsy Cellar's cuisine is (almost) a match for its atmosphere. But, no matter. You could eat gruel in a place like this and be content. The Gypsy Cellar is the type of place that make the pursuit of serendipity worthwhile. If you only visit one San Mateo county restaurant in your life, this should be it.

Hours: Tu-Su 5-11.
Cards: All major.

## RUSSIAN RENAISSANCE {Russia} (10/7=17)

5241 Geary Blvd.   San Francisco   752-8558

The lone reminder of a bygone era when more than twelve Russian restaurants did business in San Francisco, the Russian Renaissance--which was founded in Shanghai, China longer ago than most of can or would care to remember--has the distinction of having presented precisely the same menu for the past twenty years (of course, there has been a slight upward adjustment in price). With magical lights, sumptuous paintings--even on the ceiling--and waiters dressed in high-necked Russian uniforms; the ambience at the R.R. rivals that of New York's most highly acclaimed Russian establishments. Unfortunately, R.R.'s food has not weathered the passage of time quite so well; especially when one considers the significant sums the restaurant commands. The house special *chicken a la Kiev*, for example, while good, does not justify its steep price ($18.00). You'd do better with *golubtzy*--ukranian stuffed cabbage ($10.00) and an order of *plombir*--light fluffy Russian fruit ice cream.

Hours: Daily 4-11.
Cards: All major.

## VLADIMIR'S {Czech} (9/8=17)

12785 Sir Francis Drake Blvd.   Inverness   669-1021

In large midwestern metropolises like Cleveland and Chicago, fine Slavic restaurants are, if not a dime, then only about a two bits a dozen. In the West you can count such restaurants on one hand. At Vladimir's, an authentic bit of the old country implausibly located on the main drag of Inverness, small touches like waiters in traditional costumes and hot homemade Moravian rye served on a breadboard make for an authentic, homey atmosphere. To put yourself in the proper frame of mind, start with a *kava vladmir*-coffee with traditional plum brandy (*slivovitz*), whipped cream and chocolate. Then try one of Vladimir's fine Czech entrees like *chicken paprikash, svickova*--tenderloin beef in sour cream, or *Moravian cabbage roll*--with ham hocks, veal and champagne kraut. Vladimir's desserts (homemade apple strudel and chocolate cake) are also superb. Lunch is prix fixe at $8.50. Dinner--which adds soup, salad and homemade Czech dumplings--is prix fixe at $14.50.

Hours: Daily 11-11.
Cards: No.

## HUNGARIAN HUSZAR (THE) {Hungary} (9/8=17)

36601 Newark Blvd.   Newark   796-8061

    The Hungarian Huszar--the Bay Area's best Hungarian restaurant--is a cozy little place located in a hard to find Newark shopping center. It's worth seeking out, however, not only for its tastefully elegant East European decor--much of which emphasizes the Huszar (Hungarian cavalrymen) theme--but because prices for wonderful meals are rarely so low ($7.95 and up for a full course meal). Chef George Kloczl, who left his native Hungary in 1956 but revisited it in order to purchase many of the restaurant's fascinating decorations, has created a masterful menu of traditional Hungarian recipes including *gulyas* (goulash) served with *langos*--fried peasant bread ($5.95); *hideg megyleves*--cold cherry soup ($3.75--but watch out, they don't remove the pits); and traditional favorites suchr as *toltott kaposzta*--cabbage stuffed with meat ($8.95). For dessert, try the *palascinta*--Hungarian crepes ($3.50). The Huszar's ambience is further enhanced by live accordion and violin music on Saturday nights.

Hours: M-F 11:30-2; Tu-Su 5:30-9:30.
Cards: All major.

## EUGENE'S {Poland} (8/8=16)

420 San Antonio Rd.   Los Altos   941-1222

    With the recent passing of Berkeley's "Warzawa", Eugene's assumed the distinction of being the Bay Area's only Polish representative. (Actually, Pierogies Please--see below--is also Polish, but it is more of a kiosk than a restaurant). However, Eugene's carries the Polish banner well. Indeed, it is like an ethnic oasis in the otherwise arid sands of Silicon Valley. While Eugene's boasts some attractive decorations, what really makes its atmosphere special is...well, Eugene himself, the restaurant's owner, host, and sometime waiter who also turns in a very credible performance playing Polish tunes on the guitar. As far as cuisine is concerned, Eugene's serves delicious borscht and some good, hearty meat items such as homemade kielbasa. You may have had kielbasa before, out of a package or jar, but you can't say you've tasted *real* Polish kielbasa until you've experienced what homemade ingredients and fresh preparation can do.

Hours: Tu-F 11:30-2:30; Tu-Sa 5:30-10:30.
Cards: V/MC/AE.

## FONO PAPRIKAS {Hungary} (7/8=15)

900 Northpoint (Ghirardelli Sq.) San Francisco 441-1223

Lack of authentic music and Hungarian service keeps Fono Paprikas from rating higher. The restaurant itself is extremely appealing, with a gorgeous Ghirardelli bay view location. The fact that its prices are so reasonable is just one more reason to try it. Fono's specialty of the house is *goulash* (spelled *gulyas*)--the classic Hungarian meat and potato stew. You can order *gulyas* by the cup or the *bogracs*--a thin walled iron kettle which is suspended over an open fire. Another house specialty is *langos*--delicious fried peasant bread ($2.75). Authentic lunch items include *chicken strudel*--chicken cooked in sauce, chopped and rolled into strudel dough, then baked crisp ($5.95). Also available and well worth a try are assorted *palascintas*--Hungarian dessert crepes, and *profiteroles*--cream puffs with ice cream topped with hot brandied chocolate; as well as one of the Bay Area's best collections of Hungarian wines including *tokaj*--Hungarian honey wine ($2.50 per glass).

Hours: Daily 11:30-10 (exc. F-Sa until 11).
Cards: V/MC/DC.

## CAFE BOHEMIA {Czechoslovakia} (4/7=11)

514 Main St. Martinez 228-0301

Martinez, a pristine town nestled in a pretty little valley, is not usually considered to be a bastion of ethnic delights. That's why it was nice when Cafe Bohemia opened up, bringing a little of the old country to Contra Costa County. If it weren't for its name, you wouldn't suspect Cafe Bohemia as being Czech. It looks pretty much like any cafe, and you have to look hard to find those few touches of Central Europe--strips of brightly flowered wallpaper, lace curtains, a few Bohemian flower pots--that reflect the restaurant's heritage. Cafe Bohemia's lunch menu is basically standard sandwich, with token East European touches (the sandwiches are served on black bread)--but Eastern European dinners--including *znoimia goulash*--chunks of pork in a paprika sauce ($7.50)--abound. This is also one of the few places in the East Bay where you can get Pilsner Urquel (in continuous production for over 600 years, it is billed as the "world's best beer").

Hours: M-F 11-2:30; Th-Sa 6-9.
Cards: AE.

## PETROUCHKA {Russia} (7/4=11)

2930 College Ave.   Berkeley   848-7860

In addition to its pretty name, Petrouchka boasts some eye-catching Russian finery, including a small but exquisite samovar and two brightly colored shawls you could just die for. Unfortunately, you won't see anyone dressed up in a cossack outfit, no one speaks "ra-usshun", and Petrouchka's food is only fair. We go primarily for its homemade desserts such as *blinchiki s syrom*--a hot Russian crepe filled with sour cream and lemon cheese and topped with black cherry sauce ($2.50).

Hours: Daily 11-10.
Cards: V/MC.

## VLASTA'S {Czechoslovakia} (n/r)

2420 Lombard St.   San Francisco   931-7533

With items like *chicken paprikash*, sweetbreads in tarragon, and *szekely goulash*--diced pork and sour cabbage cooked in a piquant paprika sauce with sour cream, Vlasta's boasts a fairly authentic Czech menu. However, there is not much about its atmosphere to make you feel like you're visiting Brno.

Hours: Tu-Su 5:30-10.
Cards: All major.

## GELCO'S {Yugoslavia} (n/r)

1450 Lombard St.   San Francisco   928-1054

Gelco's, San Francisco's only "official" Yugoslavian restaurant (the venerable Tadich's is Yugoslav-owned but has no Yugoslav ambience), displays a few Slavic ornaments, but not enough to warrant a special trip. Also, with items like *petrale sole* and *moussaka* on its menu (which otherwise features virtually nothing but lamb), there isn't too much about Gelco's to make one pine for Dubrovnic.

Hours: M-Sa 5:30-11.
Cards: All major.

## VICKI'S PLACE {Russia} (n/r)

1823 Lombard St.   San Francisco   922-2466

Although Vicki's bills itself as "Russian-American", its emphasis is decidedly on the latter. A few Russian specialties (e.g. pelmeni, piroshki, and sometimes borscht) are served, but Vicki's has no Russian atmosphere.

Hours: Daily 7:30-3.
Cards: None.

## PEROGIES PLEASE {Poland} (n/r)

Emery Bay Public Market--5800 Shellmound   Emeryville   547-8400

Perogies are served, of course, and quite a few other East European dishes including *golobchi*--stuffed cabbage, potato pancakes and even Armenian batlajan (eggplant) as well. No East European flavor, however.

Hours: M-Th 8:30-7; F 8:30-8; Sa 9-6; Su 10-5.
Cards: No. Personal checks accepted.

## ACROPOLIS {Russia} (n/r)

5217 Geary Blvd.   San Francisco   751-9661

A restaurant-bakery with no clear-cut identity, Acropolis' atmosphere is more oriental than Russian; but a variety of Russian dishes including *sirniki* ($4.95), *piroshki* ($1.70) and *golubtsy* ($5.95) are served.

Hours: M-Sa 10:30-8; Su 10:30-7.
Cards: V/MC.

## VOLGA {Russia} (n/r)

2128 Oxford St.   Berkeley   843-3323

With a bill of fare strikingly similar to Petrouchka's, Volga is okay and comfortable, but decidedly un-Russian in its ambience.

Hours: Daily 5-9.
Cards: All major.

# THE MIDDLE EAST

## 5. THE MIDDLE EAST

*Afghanistan* • *Armenia* • *Lebanon* • *Persia* • *Turkey*

Sometimes memories of places long ago travelled seem to be utterly forgotten and then, all of a sudden, one sees a particular object or catches a whiff of a certain smell, and the whole panorama of one's past begins to unravel. When I (Richard) was in Iran (formerly Persia) in the mid-1970's, the Shah was still in power and matters were getting rather tense. You could just about smell revolution in the air. On top of this, it was Ramadan--the Moslem high holy days--a time for atonement, fasting, and rededication to Islamic duties. During Ramadan, infidels--particularly American ones--are not apt to make friends and influence people. Moreover, since during the holy days even seemingly minor infractions of the Islamic code such as eating in public can cause you to forfeit a limb, somehow I could never quite focus on the intricacies of Persian cuisine.

It wasn't until relatively recently, when the Bay Area began to experience a sort of Iranian restaurant renaissance, that I was able to experience Persian cuisine as it was meant to be savored--in a relaxed, almost meditative atmosphere. Although I had sampled some fine Persian dishes before, my first meal at a Bay Area Persian restaurant was more like a revelation then a reminiscence. More accurately, it was like getting to know things about an acquaintance you hadn't met in years. Then I re-encountered the haunting flavor of Persian "chelo"--Iran's incredibly light, fluffy and highly aromatic saffron rice--*and* all the sights, smells and tastes of Iran began to return.

If you have never experienced Persian cuisine, by all means go. Few native foods from any country big or small are as apt to leave such an indelible impression on your taste buds, or make you wonder how you managed to live without having experienced such flavors for so long. Further, with 15 Persian restaurants now operating in the Bay Area--many of which are excellent--visiting "Persia" is no longer a complicated affair.

Persian is not the only denomination of Middle Eastern cuisine available in the Bay Area. There are "traditional" Middle Eastern restaurants which showcase Lebanese and/or "Arabic" foods, and several from places like Afghanistan, Armenia and Turkey as well. While each of these cultures and cuisines are fascinating, on account of the significant disparities between them, we will discuss them in the context of the individual reviews of the restaurants which represent them. Here, we concentrate on introducing you to the alluring and often delightful cuisine of Persia.

## *Aash* (Soup), Salad and *Mazeh* (Appetizers)

Neither soup nor salad is common in Iran, but "mazeh" (appetizers) are an integral part of the Persian meal and should not be missed. Three of the most common Persian appetizers are *dolmeh*--stuffed grape leaves; *kashko bademjan*--eggplant blended with whey; and *torshi*--pickled vegetables. *Mast*--homemade yogurt--or one of its variegated forms such as *mast o khiar* (mast with cucumbers) or *mast o musir* (mast with shallots) are omnipresent and virtual must preludes to any Persian meal. In addition, most Persian restaurants serve some sort of *sabzi* (salad)--a traditional mixture of goat cheese and herbs. A few will also offer *kofteh kebabs*--meatballs made with vegetables, rice and beans.

## Entrées

Most people think of Persia as the land that gave us *shashlik*--shish kebab. But *shish* is far from the final word in kebabi (kebabs). Most Persian restaurants also serve a wide variety of beef and chicken kebabi, the most common of which are *barg*--skewered beef, *joojeh*--chicken, and *koobideh*--ground beef. *Soltani* is a popular combination--one skewer of koobideh together with one of barg. Kebabi are virtually always served on a bed of succulent chelo, with a pat of melted butter on top.

At many Persian restaurants, the specials of the house change daily--with the same special being served on the same day each week. Once you've found your favorite Persian entree, which for us is *fesenjun*--an outstanding sweet and sour chicken dish prepared with ground walnuts in pomegranate sauce--you will become accustomed to visiting the restaurant of your choice on the appointed day. Other popular Persian entrees include baghali polo--lamb shanks with lima beans; ghorme sabzi--beef, herbs and red beans; loobia polo--beef with green beans and zereshk polo--chicken breast with currants and rice.

## Beverages and Desserts

With the exception of *chai*--spiced tea, there is nothing all that special about Persian beverages. *Doogh*--a *lassi*-like yogurt concoction--is interesting but often difficult for Westerners to drink because it is so salty. Desserts are another matter. The three you are most likely to be offered at Persian restaurants are *baklawa*, *zoolbia* and akbar mashti. *Baklawa* is, of course, a honey-dipped pastry which is common not only to the whole of the Middle East and Greece, but is much loved in India as well. *Zoolbia* is a sweet pastry ring, served dripping with honey.

The premier Persian dessert, however, is the irresistible *akbar mashti*--a delightful, highly texturous honey ice cream. Another interesting Persian sweet treat, not as common, is *faloodeh*--an iced dessert made with tiny noodles. Just to show how small the world really is, one of our favorite Indian desserts, kulfi, is occasionally known by its formal name--*kulfi faluda*; and Persian *faloodeh* is sometimes referred to as "paloodeh"--*paluda* being the operative ingredient of the most popular desserts of Malaysia, Indonesia and the Philippines.

## KHAYYAM'S CHELO KABAB {Persia} (9/8=17)

1373 Solano Ave.   Albany   526-7200

Since there were, at last count, 15 Bay Area Persian restaurants--and since most Persian places feature similar decor and virtually identical menus--to excel in the Persian restaurant business you have to stand out in the subtle things. From your first glimpse of Khayyam's gently burbling fountain, you will sense that you are onto something special. Stained glass windows and brightly colored lamps lend a cheerful air to its front room, where you can while away some happy time relishing the Tabriz rugs and Persian miniature portraits which are there on permanent display. Our favorite place, however, is in the back which--in addition to other Persian amenities--boasts a skylight and gossamer hanging vines. These, together with the recent addition of hand-painted tiles, give the effect of an authentic Persian courtyard. Unlike many restaurants which close between lunchtime and dinner, Khayyam's is open all day. Our favorite time to go is during those "in between" hours when few local visitors are lollygagging about. It is then that Khayyam's is at its best. Khayyam's offers a larger selection of appetizers than most. You might consider its combination platter ($8.95), which features small portions of several, including *dolmeh*--stuffed grape leaves, and *mirza ghasemi*--mashed eggplant. *Chelo* means rice and *Kabab* meat--specifically, that succulent specimen of charbroiled meat on the skewer that Westerners have come to typically identify only with *shish* (lamb). While the *shish kabab* at Khayyam's is excellent ($9.45), each of its other kababs--*joojeh* (chicken--$8.95), *koobideh* (ground beef--$6.95) and *barg* (beef filet)--$8.45) are also worth a try. While kababs get most of the press, the thing that will bring you back to Khayyam's, again and again, is its fluffy and aromatic saffron-flavored *chelo*. If you were only going to sample one Persian entree in your life, it would have to be *khoresht fesenjone ("fesenjun")*--chicken in a thick fragrant pomegranate sauce ($6.95). Fortunately, at Khayyam's, you're not limited to trying only one Persian entree, since the restaurant offers a *combination khoresht* which gives you the opportunity to sample two other savory entrees, *gheimeh budemjone*--a cut beef and eggplant saute, and *ghormeh sabzi*--a very tasty beef stew, in addition to fesenjun, for only $9.95. For a refreshing drink try Khayyam's sour cherry juice ($1.75), not its interesting but salty yogurt concoction, *doogh* ($.75). By the way, the service at Khayyam's is marvelous.

Hours: Tu-Su: 11:30--10. Reservations Appreciated.
Cards: All major.

## ARIANA'S {Afghanistan} (7/9=16)

22449 Foothill Blvd.   Hayward   581-1118

In order for Ariana's--a small, cheerful restaurant with pink tablecloths, colorful hanging rugs and a large poster emphatically proclaiming a "Free Afghanistan"--to attract visitors to its Hayward location, it has to offer something extraordinary. It does--the widest selection of high quality Afghani food in Northern California, including a slate of dishes you're not apt to have ever tried before, all at reasonable prices. Start with *bulani potatoes*--with leeks and onions in a flour *tortilla* ($3.50). Other interesting appetizers include *ashak*--ground beef and onions boiled in thin bread ($7.95) and *manto*--basically the same, with yogurt ($7.95). Ariana's also offers some interesting entrees, most notably a host of *kebabs* like *liver kebab* ($5.95) and *dopiaza*--marinated lamb and leeks in garlic ($7.95). Araiana's wide range of desserts includes two Afghani ones-*Afghani cake* ($1.75), and *jelabi*--a flavorful honey and wheat pastry ($2.25.)

Hours: Daily: 10(a)-11.
Cards: All major.

## CHELOKABABI {Persia} (8/8=16)

1236 S. Wolfe Rd.   Sunnyvale   (408) 737-1222

Chelokababi touts itself as serving "Persian delicacy at its finest". Surprisingly, this may be one restaurant that lives up to its own billing. On your way in to a large ornate room filled with attractive Middle Eastern decorations, you pass by a couple of twittering canaries sitting one on each side of a large Persian urn. Conversation is animated, and mostly in Persian. As its name suggests (chelo=rice, kababi=meat), Chelokababi specializes in grilled meats. Of these, barg chengeh--a skewer of grilled filet mignon ($7.25) is perhaps the best, although joojeh--chicken ($6.75) is also quite good. For a liquid taste sensation, try Chelo's *cucumber juice*--a drink so refreshing you'll wonder why it isn't bottled by Coke. Chelo offers a wider selection of desserts than most Persian places, ranging from the bite-sized, honey-dipped *bamieh* ($.45) to the restaurant's piece d'resistance, *makhloot*. Makhloot combines Persian honey ice cream and *faloodeh shirazi*--an iced dessert made with noodles.

Hours: Daily 11-10.
Cards: V/MC.

## AZIZ I {Afghanistan} (8/7=15)

2075 Mountain Blvd. (Montclair Village) Oakland 339-9943

If you have come to believe, as we have, that you can measure how good an ethnic restaurant is by how much it makes you either want to go somewhere you haven't been, or return somewhere you have; Azizi is a great restaurant. Although it boasts only a few pretty Afghani rugs, as well as some of the more interesting lamp shades you'll ever see, there is something about Azizi that's puts you in the mood to travel the way few other restaurants do. But even if Azizi doesn't inspire you with wanderlust, it will still be worth the trip, if just to sample such interesting Afghani entrees as *haashak*--large shells with ground beef curry, green onions and yogurt ($4.99), and *sabzy chalow*--spinach, rice and beef ($6.99). Azizi also offers some good soups and *haash*--noodles and ground beef with beans in yogurt ($2.99). For dessert, try *Afghani ferny*--Afghanistan's equivalent to Indian *firni* ($1.50). It's good.

Hours: M-Th 11:30-9; F-Su 11:30-10.
Cards: No. No personal checks.

## CAFE MARMARA {Turkey} (7/6=13)

1730 Shattuck Ave. Berkeley 644-1966

Whenever we first visit a restaurant which is the exclusive representative of any national cuisine we get a bit nervous. If any other restaurant doesn't make it, it's no big deal; but if a "unique" restaurant fails, an entire country drops off the Bay Area culinary map. Fortunately Cafe Marmara, the Bay Area's only Turkish haunt, appears like its going to survive. While its service isn't authentic, its decor--with some huge Turkish pictures and a couple of nice kilim rugs--isn't bad. Marmara's fare, too, is pretty on target with all the best loved items from your last trip to Istanbul; such as *böreks*--Turkish stuffed filo dough pies ($8.25--$8.75), and *imam bayildi*--stuffed baked eggplant ($8.75); as well as some you're not apt to have tasted before like *firinda ferik*--roast game hen with bulgur wheat and Anatolian spices ($10.75). The items we like best are Marmara's two eggplant *mezeler* (appetizers)--*patlican tava*--fried eggplant with yogurt, and *patlican ezme*--eggplant puree (both $3.75).

Hours: M-Sa 6-10.
Cards: AE/DC. Personal checks accepted.

## MAYKADEH {Persia} (5/8=13)

470 Green St.   San Francisco   362-8286

    Good, but not great, the ambience at Maykadeh is more French than Persian, with plenty of modern lights and lots of glass. The only Iranian touch is provided by the music. Unlike Maykadeh's decor, its food is Persian with a capital "P". Unfortunately, even here there are some unnecessary Western accommodations. For example, several entrees are cooked over mesquite. Particularly recommended is *joojeh kabab*--boneless chicken marinated in homemade yogurt and saffron ($7.50). Maykadeh also offers daily specials, perhaps the best of which is *khoresht bademjun*--eggplant braised with lamb shank, tomatoes and dried lime. Dessert is not a strong points at Maykadeh, but it does serve traditional Iranian *chai* in a tall glass. This is also a good place to try *doogh*, Iran's salty equivalent of Indian *lassi*. The elements of a trip are here, but Maykadeh seems a bit too concerned with accommodating western tastes, instead of giving us a demonstration of the uniqueness of theirs.

Hours: M-F 11:30-2:30, 5-11; Sa-Su 1-11.
Cards: V/MC.

## MIDDLE EAST (THE) {Lebanon} (6/7=13)

2125 University Ave.   Berkeley   549-1926

    There is not all that much to the decor at the Middle East--a few nice gold platters, a sword, lots of mirrors--but there is a certain Mediterranean feel about the place; and friendly, enthusiastic service makes up for a lot. Foodwise, there is no questioning the Middle East's cultural integrity. A full slate of fine Middle Eastern *mezza* (appetizers), salads and entrees are offered. Of the Middle East's appetizers, its *fool madammas*--Egyptian fava beans ($3.25) and *labneh*--cream of yogurt ($3.25) are probably the best. Its *baba ghannouj*--smoked eggplant ($3.25) is only fair, as is its *tabouleh*--a traditional Lebanese salad made from bulgur wheat, olive oil, herbs and lemon ($3.50). For your main course, we'd recommend *shish tawook*--broiled chicken breast on a skewer ($7.95) and *kibby*--cracked wheat mixed with ground lamb and pine nuts ($7.50). For dessert? Baklawa, what else? ($1.50).

Hours: Tu-Su 11:30-2, 5-9:30. F-Sa until 10:30.
Cards: No.

## JUST LIKE HOME {Middle East} (6/6=12)

1924 Irving St.   San Francisco   681-3337

What with a three dimensional pyramid mural, mournful Arabic music, and pictures of Palestinian cities, this isn't just like anyone's home *we* know, but that's what gives Just Like Home its charm. This cafeteria-style haunt is one of the few places in the city where you can savor such unusual delicacies as *tohalat*--stuffed lamb spleens. For dessert, try a date or walnut *mamoul*--not exactly a cookie, not exactly a cake ($1.00), but very good, especially with some (strong) Arabic coffee ($.85).

Hours: M-Sa 10-10.
Cards: No. Cash only.

## KABUL {Afghanistan} (5/8=13)

833 W. El Camino Real   Sunnyvale   (408) 245-4350

Superior cuisine at this justifiably popular Afghani haunt in a small South Peninsula shopping center. The restaurant's problem is that it is formal to the point of being austere--a fact incongruous with its Afghani heritage. If Kabul loosened up a bit, and gave more than a passing nod to the decor and traditions of its country of origin, this could be one of the Bay Area's top twenty ethnic restaurants of any kind.

Hours: Su-Th 11-2; 5:30-10; F-Sa 5:30-11.
Cards: V/MC.

## SUNRISE DELI {Arabia} (6/6=12)

2115 Irving St.   San Francisco   (415) 664-8210

Sunrise Deli features similar fare to "Just Like Home" in a slightly funkier, but equally authentic, locale. Surprise specialties include *Armenian Pizza*--with ground lamb, tahini and pine nuts ($1.55) and *maza*--hoummous with tabouli on pita bread ($3.45). This is also one of the best places in the Bay Area for *shawarma* ($3.99). A wide variety of authentic Middle Eastern sweets are available.

Hours: M-Sa 8:30(a)-9(p); Su 10-7.
Cards: No.

## KASRA {Persia} (4/8=12)

349 Clement St. San Francisco 752-1101

Kasra is one of the city's fancier Persian restaurants but little, apart from its menu, distinguishes it as being Persian. Try *bademjan*--beef and eggplant in tomato sauce ($7.50).

Hours: M-Th 11:30-10; F-Su 1-11.
Cards: All major.

## PAPA'S {Persia} (4/6=10)

2026 University Ave. Berkeley 841-0884

Papa's is clean and cozy but undistinguished. Its food, decor and service are all adequate but unspectacular, and there are no innovative items on its menu. Not a bad place for take out.

Hours: M, W-F 11:30-11; Sa-Su 12-11.
Cards: V/MC/AE.

## HAIG'S DELICACIES {Middle East} (n/r)

642 Clement St. San Francisco 752-6283

Really a Middle Eastern sundry shop, not a restaurant, but Haig's walls are nicely adorned with Middle Eastern prints, its smells are lovely, and this is as nice a place as any to linger over a cup of Arabic coffee.

Hours: M-Sa 10-6.
Cards: V/MC.

## ARMENIAN GOURMET {Armenia} (n/r)

929 E. Duane Ave. Sunnyvale (408) 732-3910

Stained glass and beer signs give no hint of ethnic ambience or culture at this long-established Armenian South Peninsula tradition.

Hours: M-F 11-1:30; W-F 5:30-9.
Cards: All major.

## MEDITERRANEAN GARDENS {Middle East} (n/r)

809 San Pablo Ave.  Albany  526-8014

We can overlook things like boring decor (framed travel posters) and inattentive service, but there isn't much else to make this one feel Middle Eastern. It's often crowded, however, so it must be doing something right.

Hours: Daily 5-10.
Cards: All major.

## YAS CAFE {Persia} (n/r)

822 Irving St.  San Francisco  664-5113

Yas bills itself as an American *and* Persian but a lone Middle Eastern painting and a couple of mediocre Persian dishes are all that sets Yas from a typical American coffee shop.

Hours: Daily 7(a)-10(p).
Cards: None.

## DELI EATS {Middle East} (n/r)

86 McAllister St.  San Francisco  864-3304

When we last visited in July 1989, Deli Eats was planning to "upgrade" its Middle Eastern menu. No plans were in the works to give the place an ethnic feel, however, which presently is non-existent.

Hours: M-F 8-9; Sa-Su 8-5.
Cards: None.

## MIRACLE MILE CAFE {Middle East} (n/r)

2998 Mission St.  San Francisco  285-4028

Formerly the Jerusalem Cafe, the Miracle Mile came under new (non-Middle Eastern) ownership since we were there last. We'll let you know.

Hours: M-Sa 9-6.
Cards: No. No personal checks.

# AFRICA

## 6. AFRICA

*Algeria • Egypt • Eritrea • Ethiopia • Morocco • Tunisia*

Although Africa is a large continent with dozens of independent nations, when one thinks of African cuisine, two regions--North Africa and East Africa--come to mind. These in turn--to most people at least--boil down to Morocco and Ethiopia. Actually, while many Bay Area North African restaurants are purely Moroccan, some serve dishes from several other North African nations including Algeria, Tunisia and Egypt.

Similarly, while Ethiopia dominates the Bay Area's East African restaurant scene, a few of the area's better East African restaurants are actually not from Ethiopia, but *Eritrea*--Eritrea being the Red Sea coastal state embroiled in a seemingly endless war with the Ethiopian government. In this chapter, we will first take a look at some of the more common and interesting dishes and desserts of North Africa, then at the cuisine served at some of the Bay Area's many fine East African representatives.

## North Africa

**Algeria • Egypt • Morocco • Tunisia**

At many North African restaurants one gets the feeling that the emphasis is on maintaining an exotic and appealing atmosphere--which usually means belly-dancing--rather than on the restaurant's rendition of genuine North African fare. This is a shame because, for an area with a small population, North Africa has developed a fairly sophisticated indigenous cuisine.

### Appetizers

Most North African restaurants are only open for dinner and, with few exceptions, are *"prix fixe"* affairs which offer little choice of anything except perhaps entrees. At such restaurants, prior to your main course you are usually served three dishes: *harira*--lentil soup, *mechouia*--a vegetable and olive oil mixture which is called a "salad" but contains no lettuce, and *bestella*--a heavenly combination of chicken, almonds and sugar baked in filo dough. Although being served these same three items (in slightly altered form) again and again might lead you to conclude that they constitute the sum total of all North African hors d'oeuvres, there are actually quite a few other appetizers enjoyed in the region. *Bourak*, a tasty filo pie *derived from the Turkish borek*, is one of these. Others include *coca*--sauteed vegetables in a baked dough, *brik*--the same type of dough with eggs and tuna, and *merguez*--a spicy lamb and beef sausage. You may also come across two additional North African soups: *frik*--spicy cracked wheat in broth, and *chorba m'kefta*--a hearty herb stew.

## The Main Course

At many North African restaurants, the house specialty, and rightly so, is *couscous*--a coarse, gritty but highly flavorful grain which is eaten in conjunction with all sorts of meats and vegetables but, most often, lamb or chicken. At Moroccan restaurants, your other choices are apt to be braised chicken, hare, or a variety of *l'ham* (lamb) dishes--possibly served with almonds, dried fruits or *kamama*--with honey and onions.

At other North African restaurants, you may be served *chicken tadjin*--baked with lemon, olives and mushrooms; l'ham *loubia*--designating the type of beans cooked with the lamb; or a lamb dish more routinely associated with Persia--shish kebab. While North African restaurants are not particularly well known for their desserts, they are justifiably famous for their mint tea and, especially, for the graceful way in which it is poured over a small glass from great height.

## ALI'S {North Africa, Middle East} (9/8=17)

385 Colusa Ave. Kensington 526-1500

Perhaps the best word to describe both the atmosphere and cuisine of Ali's is "eclectic". With some of this and a little of that from virtually every country in North Africa and the Middle East, Ali's could properly be described as either a traditional North African restaurant with a heavy Middle Eastern influence, or a traditional Middle Eastern restaurant, with a pronounced North African accent. The first thing you notice at Ali's are a couple of pretty paintings in the classic Egyptian mummy design. Inside Ali's cavernous main dining room, you will observe a room divided. On one side are the traditional low tables, cushions and stools of Morocco. On the other side is a more formal area of tables and chairs which looks much like what you would expect to see in a nice restaurant in Damascus or Amman. Ali's stocks wines from Tunisia and Algeria, its chef is from Iraq, and, if you are familiar with Middle Eastern and North African cuisine, you will notice that Ali's menu features everything from "a to z", as in Middle Eastern *arnab*--braised rabbit in paprika sauce ($15.50), to *zaalouk*--Moroccan pureed eggplant ($4.50); with representative offerings from just about every country in between. Unlike other restaurants which attempt to blend diverse cultures and cuisines into a homogenous whole, Ali's succeeds admirably in capturing the feeling of a large and important part of two continents without trivializing the contribution of any one country in the process. For example, Ali's offers a delightful *merguez*-- spicy grilled lamb sausage, a traditional Tunisian appetizer ($4.75); a side order of Algerian *couscous*--a gritty grain most commonly associated with Algeria ($2.00); Lebanese *fettouch*--romaine lettuce with feta cheese and tomatoes tossed in olive oil ($4.50); and even Saudi Arabian *tagine*-- braised lamb with okra and tomato ($16.50). At many Moroccan restaurants, you will be entertained by a belly dancer who will periodically interrupt your meal to wriggle and gyrate, sometimes beckoning you to dance, and always hoping you will press some greenbacks into her (or his) wildly gyrating hip pockets. While Ali's also features belly dancing, here entertainment is limited to brief performances which are truly that--more art than a method of arousal. The other thing that distinguishes the entertainment at Ali's is that live music is played throughout the night. Indeed, this is probably one of the few restaurants in the United States where you can enjoy a live performance on the *kanoon*--a Middle Eastern instrument reminiscent of the zither--while you dine.

Hours: Daily from 5-11.
Cards: V/MC/AE.

## EL MOROCCO {Morocco} (9/7=15)

1311 Meadow Lane   Concord   671-0132

Probably about the last place you'd expect to find an authentic North African eatery would be two doors down from the "screw shop" in a back road, four store shopping center in Concord. However, if you want to experience the pleasure of visiting "El Morocco"--the East Bay's only Moroccan restaurant--that's where you have to go. Once inside, you'll observe two things: soft multi-colored Turkish lights and rich oriental rugs. As your eyes begin to adjust to the light, you'll notice something more: instead of chairs, the seats are stools and cushions and, instead of tables, your food is served on ornate golden trays. As at most Moroccan restaurants, all courses except your entree are pre-selected. Your meal begins with the ceremonial cleansing of the hands, then you are offered a steaming bowl of *harira*--an interesting hot lentil soup. Next you are served a tray of *mahgreb salad*--pureed eggplant with tomatoes and spices. Up next is *bastila*--the showcase North African filo pie stuffed with chicken, almonds, spices--and lots of sugar. The bastila here is not quite as tasty as at some other local Moroccan haunts, but it is hot and tangy. El Morocco offers a wider choice of entrees than most Moroccan restaurants. Among the possibilities are cornish hen, beef brochette, *braised hare, and* several lamb dishes, including lamb with prunes or *kamana*--with honey and onions. We prefer couscous, however, with either chicken or vegetables. After another hand washing, you reach the final food course--a fairly bland Moroccan honey nut pastry and mint tea, which is served in ceremonial fashion, from high above the glass. As with most Moroccan restaurants, the meal does not end here. The final course (and primary attraction) is belly dancing. However, unlike at some restaurants, where customers are obligated to drop whatever they are doing either to press money into the waistband of a writhing body of whatever gender or, sometimes, to get up and writhe along; belly dancing at El Morocco can be either participatory or spectatorial, as you choose. This allows both extrovert and introvert to conclude their meal in perfect contentment. While you might expect that the tab for what is, in effect, a meal and an exotic show would be quite steep, at El Morocco the prix fixe is only $16.95 per person. This is a lot less than you might pay at some "regular" restaurants with no atmosphere for just an entree, dessert and a cup of joe. El Morocco's exotic decor alone just about justifies its price. The food and show almost seem like they're thrown in.

Hours: W-Sa 5:30-11; Su 4:30-11.
Cards: All major.

## MAMOUNIA {Morocco} (9/7=16)

200 Merrydale Rd.   San Rafael   472-1372

Tents, carpets, colors, waiters and waitresses in native garb--Mamounia really does a job of transporting you. If you like belly dancing, Mamounia has it. If you are into quiet conversation in a relaxed setting, you will be seated in a sumptuous and semi-private back room. Plus, at Mamounia, unlike at some other Moroccan restaurants which put a premium on glitz, the magic is not lost on the food. Although at Mamounia, as at other North African restaurants, the only choice you are given is between entrees, you will not feel slighted. This is because all meals come with Mamounia's delicious *harira*, bestella pie and spiced tea. Mamounia also features one of the Bay Area's best selection of Moroccan wines. Although prices are steep (about $22.50 per person), you won't mind, because Mamounia is not just an ordinary restaurant. Mamounia also has a San Francisco location at 4411 Balboa (752-6566). At both restaurants, reservations are recommended.

Hours: Th-Su 6-10.
Cards: V/AE/MC. No personal checks accepted.

## CASBAH {Algeria, Tunisia} (7/9=16)

1920 San Pablo Ave.   Berkeley   540-0784

Casbah has a "year of the cat" atmosphere featuring soft lights, a ceiling cloth and soothing music which gives one the sense that they are travelling for real. Although not as chic as--say--Mamounia, Casbah is inviting in its own way; and its surprisingly diverse cuisine is superb. Uncommon appetizers like *brik*--tuna and egg baked in crispy dough ($3.50), and *coca*--baked dough filled will vegetables ($2.50), set the stage for Casbah's traditional couscous entrees, or a variety of *tadjins*. At $9.00, Casbah's *chicken tadjin*--a half chicken baked with mushrooms, lemon and a riot of olives in a spicy sauce--is one of the most innovative entrees you will be served for under $10.00 anywhere in the Bay Area. A variety of lamb dishes and *dolma*--zucchini stuffed with vegetables and beef in a light sauce ($12.00) are also very good. From a purely culinary standpoint, Casbah's only shortcoming is its lack of a good, authentic North African dessert.

Hours: Tu-Su 5:30-10:30.
Cards: V/MC/AE.

## CAIRO CAFE  {Egypt}  (7/8=15)

104 Strawberry Village   Mill Valley   389-1101

Any time a restaurant is the only representative of a particular country's cuisine and ambience, we cross our fingers and hope that it is authentic and good enough to survive. Fortunately, the Cairo Cafe, at present Northern California's only Egyptian exponent, has all the earmarks of a success. Ceiling fans, Egyptian prints and gorgeous tablecloths in a familiar Egyptian mummy design combine with pleasant Egyptian music and superior service to afford an authentic Nile Delta experience. As befits a "one of a kind" restaurant, Cairo Cafe features many exotic dishes, including some you won't find elsewhere like "Alexandra Midrammis"--Egyptian fava beans, garlic and spices ($4.95). The Cafe also offers some beguiling desserts (try its baked rice pudding--$2.50). Cairo's tiny (no table seats more than four) rear-end of shopping center location hurts, but if you look you will find it; and the Cairo is definitely worth looking for. Belly dancing is performed on Friday and Saturday evenings.

Hours: Tu-Sa 11-10; Su 12(n)-9.
Cards: V/MC/AE.

## EL MAHGREB  {Morocco}  (6/6=12)

145 W. Santa Clara Ave.   San Jose   (408) 294-2243

One of San Jose's most popular nightspots, the primary attraction at El Mahgreb, as at many North African restaurants, is belly dancing. This is a shame since, during performances, the atmosphere of the restaurant, otherwise appealing, can take on a circus-like air. El Mahgreb has beautiful, exotic decor and, while its food--the same basic prix fixe dinner offered elsewhere (see review of "El Morocco")--is pretty good and pleasantly served, it can be hard to enjoy even a perfect bestella when some highly oiled, half-naked person is writhing in your face, daring you to insert a greenback of whatever denomination into you know where.

Hours: Daily 5:30-10.
Cards: V/MC/AE

# EAST AFRICA

*Eritrea • Ethiopia*

Possibly no group of local ethnic establishments rate such consistently high marks for decor and good service as do the region's numerous and growing number of fine East African ones; an inordinate percentage of which are located in the same city--Oakland, and even on the same avenue--Telegraph; which may well boast more East African eateries than any other street west of Nairobi.

While East African fare can also be good it is, perhaps, the most difficult of all ethnic cuisines for Americans to become accustomed to. This is so primarily because of the many spices--mostly unfamiliar to Americans--which are employed in preparing East African foods. Chief among these are *berbere*--a combination of spices heavily accented by red pepper; *abesh*--a spice akin to *fenugreek; gomman*--Ethiopian cabbage seeds: *zingibel*--dried ginger; and *rock salt*.

Another thing that makes dining in East African restaurants a bit disconcerting for some Americans is the way the food is traditionally eaten--without silverware. In Ethiopia, the family typically sits around a large woven basket-table called a *mesob*, sharing foods served on a large plate set in the mesob's center. While wooden spoons are sometimes used, forks and knives are not. Many local East African restaurants remain true to this tradition, although most will politely provide you with silverware if you absolutely cannot make the transition.

## Appetizers

Appetizers are not particularly common in East Africa so the items that appear under the appetizer heading on some East African menus, particularly in Eritrean restaurants, tend to be appropriations from other lands. For example, you might be offered *tabouli*--a bulgur wheat "salad" with garnish and spices, or *homous*--ground garbanzo beans with lemon juice, olive oil and garlic. Both of these are more commonly associated with the Middle East than with East Africa. Or you might be offered a *sambusa*. This is the Ethiopian lentil and green pepper equivalent of Indian *samosa*. On occasion you will notice that an East African restaurant may offer *bademjone*. This dish--made from eggplant, yogurt, lemon juice and garlic--is an East African adaptation of Persian *bademjun*.

### Entrées

In East African restaurants, there is a heavy emphasis on vegetarian cooking. In some restaurants, in fact, vegetarian offerings outnumber meat ones. Of East Africa's divers vegetarian possibilities, some of the best are *shiro*--a warm roast split and chick pea combination, sometimes eaten with *hamlee*--green mustard; *gomen*--chopped green vegetables with garlic; and *timtimo*--split peas and lentils with onions and tomatoes. Reflecting the influence of nearby Egypt, some East African restaurants may also offer *fatta*--vegetables and spices in yogurt, or *fool*--an interesting dish made from cooked Egyptian fava beans and yogurt.

Ethiopia's national dish, and one of the most popular at East African restaurants here, is *doro wat*--tender cooked chicken in chili pepper sauce, sometimes garnished with hard boiled eggs. Doro wat rarely appears on Eritrean menus, however. Instead, you might see *kitfo*--steak tartare; *kilwa*--sauteed chunks of beef with onions and peppers; and/or *zizil tibs*--sauteed beef with vegetables. Finally, as history buffs know, Ethiopia labored for a time as Italy's sole colony. Due to the colonial influence, to this day some East African restaurants serve a large assortment of Italian entrees.

### Other Items

Possibly the single most important word in the East African culinary vocabulary is *injera*--Ethiopia's fermented and therefore slightly acrid national bread. Injera is served with virtually every Ethiopian dish, and is commonly offered in Eritrean restaurants too, although these sometimes substitute *pitta*--the Middle Eastern flat bread more familiar to Americans. Another word you will see on many East African menus is *tej (taj)*. This is Ethiopia's national honey wine. Since there are numerous tribal groups in East Africa, many of which have developed their own brand of *tej*, you may see honey wine referred to by other names as well, such as *mies*--which means the same thing in Asmaric.

## BLUE NILE {Ethiopia} (9/7=16)

2525 Telegraph Ave.   Berkeley   540-6777

There is no way around the fact that African cuisine, especially East African cuisine, is an acquired taste. Few people who walk into an East African restaurant for the first time will be prepared to go back the next day. It's just too different. One places that may whet your appetite for East African food, however, is the Blue Nile. With its beads and bamboo-thatched booths--its wall hanging, murals, blinking colored lights, candles, and bamboo-framed travel posters--the Blue Nile is worth a plane ticket almost all by itself. Its food, which is standard Ethiopian (insofar as Ethiopian food can ever be called "standard") is also very good. Unlike some Ethiopian restaurants that attempt to accommodate Western tastes, at the Blue Nile you can forget about silverware--none will be offered. If you want to savor the true experience, you'll have to learn to scoop up the food with traditional doughy Ethiopian injera bread and just eat--very human. If there are two or more of you, your best bet is to split the Blue Nile's two combination dinners. B*eyayinoto* is a combination meat and chicken dish ($5.95). The Blue Nile's vegetarian combination (also $5.95) features such items as *yekik wat, split pea wat, kinche*--cracked wheat porridge, *gomen*--mustard greens steamed in a special sauce, Ethiopian rice, and salad. The *kinche* at the Blue Nile is bland but has a nice texture, while its mustard greens (*gomen wat*) are hot--very hot. Of the Blue Nile's non-vegetarian offerings, perhaps the best is *ye siga tibs*--strips of beef simmered in sauce. *Alecha*--mild curried beef stew, is also good, as is the Blue Nile's rendering of *doro wat*--chicken stew, Ethiopia's national dish. We are also partial to *kitfo*--the Ethiopian version of steak tartare. All entrees are $5.45 and are served with rice, salad, mixed vegetables and, of course, injera. Since a single entree of any of these alone would run you $5.25, you might as well order the combination and give yourself a chance to discover which dish you like best. For drinks, in addition to ubiquitous Ethiopian honey wine, *tej* ($1.50), the Blue Nile offers a number of "health" drinks which taste a bit like Mexican licuados. These may not be particularly African, but they are sure good.

Hours: Daily 11:30-10, exc. Su 5-10.
Cards: V/MC.

## RED SEA {Ethiopia} (9/7=16)

684 N. First St. San Jose (408) 993-1990

So close to downtown San Jose and yet half a world away is the Red Sea, one of the best of the extraordinary crop of East African restaurants which dot the Bay. Located off the beaten track in a Spanish-style house, The Red Sea lulls you with hypnotic music and literally hundreds of East African basket carvings, statues and mats. Virtually everywhere you turn you will find intriguing East African objets d'art bidding you welcome. Other assets of the Red Sea are above average service and an unusually wide range of authentic Ethiopian specialties. We must admit that, while we've always been interested in visiting Ethiopian restaurants, we've never had a burning desire to travel to the country from which they hail. One trip to the Red Sea, however--with its charming decor and tranquil mien--was enough to make us reconsider our long-range vacation plans. The Red Sea is not only among the Bay Area's best East African restaurants, it is one of the top ethnic places of any kind in or near San Jose.

Hours: M-Sa 11-2; 5-9.
Cards: MC/V.

## DAHLAK {Eritrea} (8/8=16)

921 Duane Ave. Sunnyvale (408) 732-8444

Dahlak--a set of Red Sea islands where many Eritrean political prisoners are kept--is something of a symbol for the Eritrean people. The restaurant Dahlak is also a symbol--it symbolizes what restaurant going should be, but usually isn't--a place to experiment with new foods, relax, learn, enjoy and--well--travel. Dahlak's decor is simple, but you can get a good feel for Eritrea by engaging in a tete a tete with its staff, who are eager to talk to visitors about the political situation in their native land, as well as the intricacies of and differences between Ethiopian and Eritrean cuisine. Foodwise, Dahlak is like a travel of the taste buds. For a vegetarian entree, try *timtimo*--split peas and lentils in tomato sauce ($3.00). For a meat dish, all but the most hearty will want to pass on *dulet*--the traditional Eritrean dish of lamb tripe and liver ($5.50), in favor of *zignie*--finely chopped beef in blended chili pepper with spiced butter ($5.50), or *alicha*--curried lamb ($6.50).

Hours: M-F 11:30-2; Th-Sa 5:30-9:30.
Cards: V/MC/AE.

## CAFE ERITREA D'AFRIQUE {Eritrea} (8/6 =14)

4069 Telegraph Ave. Oakland 547-4520

A very ordinary front room--so ordinary in fact that an (almost) life-size poster of Manute Bol stares at you while you eat--gives way to a fancy, lovely fresh flower-filled back room. In addition to Manute, Cafe Eritrea's front room is dominated by a bookshelf filled with reading material and a sign encouraging patrons to let mind and body "grow together" by eating and reading at the same time. (How many restaurants nowadays encourage you to do that?). The Cafe's food is more Arabic than Ethiopian, with a heavy emphasis on items like *tabouly, humus, and phool*--fava beans. Our favorite is a combination of *kilwa*--sauteed beef with vegetables, and *shehan phool*--fava beans with similar ingredients and yogurt. Possibly unique to Cafe Eritrea's menu is *empotito* ($2.75)--a french bread sandwich made with potato slices, onion and tomato. Also try a fresh fruit drink such as *pineapple cream* ($1.95), made with crushed pineapples, milk and honey. Live folklore music is played on weekends.

Hours: M-F 9:30(a)-11(p); Sa-Su 11-11.
Cards: No checks accepted.

## ZULA RESTAURANT {Ethiopia} (8/6=14)

4929 Shattuck Ave. Oakland 654-2830

At first glance, Zula looks like a regular bar, but this gives way to a fine thatched dining room, adorned by stunning folk art, that seems more like a museum than a place to dine. Zula's food is unusually spicy, even by East African standards. Certain dishes--like its heavily spiced yogurt and mustard concoction known as "sefitch"--you are likely to find nowhere else. Other items are more familiar, but not by their names. For example, the common East African honey wine, tej, is known here as "mies"--which is what tej is called in Asmaric--a dialect spoken in the north of Ethiopia. As with most East African places, prices at Zula are eminently reasonable, with whole meals for two starting at under $15.00. For that price, two can share a vegetarian and non-vegetarian combination which, basically, allows you to sample it all. East African breakfast is also available at Zula, as are lunch specials which begin at $3.50.

Hours: M 5-10; Tu-Th 11:30-10; F-Su 12(n)-11.
Cards: AE.

## SHEBA RESTAURANT {Ethiopia} (8/6=14)

3109 Telegraph Ave.  Oakland  654-3741

You can learn a lot about people from the foods they eat, and one of the most enjoyable things about "travel dining" is discovering a link between places you would never have imagined. To be found on the menu of Sheba are *tabouleh* ($3.50) and *hummus* ($2.00), which are generally associated with the Middle East; and *sambusa* ($1.50)--a lentil variation of the Indian *samosa*. The real shocker, however, is *bademjone*--eggplant blended with yogurt and garlic ($2.00), normally a mainstay of the Persian diet. And for dessert, what else? Baklava! ($1.00), delicious with a little Ethiopian coffee ($.80). The rest of Sheba's menu, which ranges from $5.00--$7.00, is traditional Ethiopian. Folk art and native dresses line the walls in its main dining room. Excellent music and service enhance what is already a superior atmosphere. Sheba may not be as exotic as the Blue Nile, but it is an authentic and wonderful little place in its own right.

Hours: M 5-10; Tu-Th 11:30-11; F-Sa 11:30-11; Su 11:30-10.
Cards: V/MC.

## NYALA'S {Ethiopia} (4/7=11)

39 Grove St.  San Francisco  861-0788

One of the interesting things about Nyala's menu is that, in addition to the usual assortment of traditonal Ethiopian dishes, you will also find a full line of Italian entrees cooked in the Ethiopian style. This is attributable to the fact that, for many years, Ethiopia labored as Italy's exclusive colony. Since you can eat Italian anytime, we'd recommend that you stick to Nyala's Ethiopian offerings, particularly *doro wat*--the Ethiopian national dish. Doro wat can be made with many different ingredients. At Nyala, it is served with leg of chicken, egg, salad, cooked vegetables and sour cream on a bed of injera bread. Also worth a try are *tibs*--cubes of beef sauteed garlic butter, and *kitfo*--lean chopped beef with spices served with homemade cottage cheese (Ethiopian steak tartare). Lunch prices are quite reasonable ($4.50--$5.50). Dinners are somewhat higher. Nyala's food is good but, be forewarned, as at many other African restaurants, you are expected to eat with your hands.

Hours: M-F 11-11; Sa-Su 3-11.
Cards: V/MC.

## RASSELAS {Ethiopia} (n/r)

2801 California St.   San Francisco   567-5010

    Larger, more imposing, but decidedly less authentic than its East Bay counterparts, Rassellas is better known for its live jazz and blues than for its Ethiopian victuals.

Hours: Su-Th 11:30-10; F-Sa 11:30-11.
Cards: All major.

# INDIA

## 7. INDIA

Perhaps the most exotic flight leg of any around the world travel is the one which takes you from Nairobi to Bombay. It is a route that has been plied by Arabic traders for thousands of years and, in reverse, marks the path of migration which brought thousands of Indian nationals to East Africa. Now you too can make this trip, symbolically, without leaving Northern California. Come with us, this way, as we begin our culinary exploration of the Indian Subcontinent--perhaps the most exotic and enticing region in the world.

### India and Its Cuisine

Considering the enormous size of the country and the grandeur of its cuisine, India has yet to have the same sort of impact on the American restaurant scene that countries like China, France, Italy and even Mexico have--with two notable exceptions. These are New York City--where whole neighborhoods could be mistaken for parts of Delhi or Bombay-- and Northern California. While in the Bay Area there is (with the possible exception of a small Indian community in the vicinity of University and San Pablo Avenues in Berkeley), no specific area you can go which is certain to remind you of India, there are certainly a large and ever-growing number of places to become acquainted with the fundamentals of Indian culture and cuisine.

Despite the fact that there are now more than 60 Bay Area Indian restaurants, Indian cuisine remains a complete unknown to many. Even those who have been initiated into the culinary arts of India are rarely aware of the extraordinary diversity of subcontinental fare. Indeed, what most Americans have come to think of as the sum total of Indian cookery is, in reality, merely a representative sampling of the cuisine of Northern India, from whence the plupart of Indian immigrants to this country hail.

The Indian subcontinent is, however, quite vast. It stretches for thousands of miles from the Khyber Pass in the Northwest to the Island of Sri Lanka (formerly Ceylon) in the Southeast. As with any region so large, there are significant regional variations; and the Bay Area--which boasts several South Indian and Pakistani restaurants, as well as representatives of cities like Bombay, Calcutta, and Madras--is as good a place as any in the country to explore the subtleties of Indian regional cuisine.

While in this introduction we will focus primarily on the cuisine of North India, leaving a discussion of regional variations to individual reviews, a brief overview of the major Indian styles of cooking available here may be in order. South Indian cooking, in particular, has seemed to come into its own of late, and there are a whole host of local establishments which specialize in it.

Although the primary staple of Northern India is wheat, in South India it is rice, and rice-based dishes form the cornerstone of the South Indian diet. The most common South Indian offerings are *idlis*, *dosas* and *utappam*. Idli is a popular steamed rice-flour cake, often served with coconut chutney. Dosas are crisp ground rice and lentil crepes, often stuffed with curried vegetables. Utappam is a thicker crepe made with an onion and chili batter.

While both North and South Indian foods tend to be spicy and hot, many Pakistani and Kashmiri dishes are mild and delicate; with the emphasis on dried fruits, nuts and gentle spices like nutmeg. In Gujerati cuisine the spotlight is on vegetarian delights like *patra*--spicy fried taro root; *bhajias*--vegetables fried in garbanzo bean batter; and *dhokra*--garbanzo bean sponge cake. *Bhel poori*, a Bombay innovation, is a crunchy puffed snack containing cereal grains, onion, chili, tamarind sauce, yogurt, coriander and chutney. Finally, *vindaloo*--a hot and spicy curry sauce--was contributed to Indian cuisine by the Portuguese settlers who colonized the southwest Indian province of Goa.

### Salads and *Shorba* (Soups)

We spent more than two months in India without ever encountering anything that remotely resembled a salad. Since, in addition, we visited a couple dozen Indian restaurants on the East Coast before we came across one that included salad on its menu, we think it is safe to conclude that salad is not a mainstay of the Indian diet. However this is California, where even junk food restaurants serve salad, and some indefatigable Indian entrepreneurs have begun to offer this as an accommodation to Western tastes. However, as you contentedly munch health-giving greens at your favorite Indian establishment, keep in mind that there is really no such thing as an authentic Indian green salad. At best, in parts of Northern India and Pakistan, you might sometimes come across a mixture of chopped cucumbers, tomatoes, onions and cilantro known as "*kachumbar*".

Soups are another matter. Indians do eat them, and are quite capable of making good ones, though you may have trouble believing this if you never leave the West Coast. If local Indian restaurants serve soup at all, the soup of choice will almost *always be dal--split lentils, the same* dish which, as a side order, accompanies virtually every North Indian meal. Lentil soup can be a delight if it is made right but, unfortunately, this does not often happen here. Once in a great while you may also come across a nice tomato shorba and, in South Indian restaurants, you may be able to try a thick, spicy dal variation known as *sambar*; but that's about it. This is a shame because in many Indian restaurants on the East Coast and in London you will routinely be served delicious homemade coconut or, less frequently, chicken soup.

## *Shuruaat* (Appetizers)

While for some ethnic groups appetizers are at best an afterthought, for Indians they are a must. The most common of these are samosas--crisp, sometimes spicy, turnovers stuffed with vegetables or meat, and pakoras--vegetable (usually onion) fritters cooked in a garbanzo bean batter. Both are usually served with at least a couple of different sauces, two of which being the tamarind-based *tamarack* and mint. Some restaurants will also serve *aloo chat*--a cold, spicy combination of potatoes and vegetables; *aloo tikki*--fried potato patties stuffed with spiced lentils; and/or a variety of broiled meat *kebabs*.

## *Bhojan* (Dinners)

Since orthodox Hindus do not eat beef, Indian restaurants rarely serve it. Pork dishes--taboo to the Muslim minority--are, if anything, even more uncommon. Virtually every Indian restaurant does, however, offer a choice of three types of non-vegetarian dishes: *gosht*--lamb, *samandar*--seafood, and *murgh*--chicken. In addition, many will feature a wide variety of *sabzi bhandar*--vegetarian specialties. But what most distinguishes Indian cookery is not so much the type of food served as the method by which it is prepared. The two Indian styles of food preparation you are most likely to encounter are "curry" and "tandoori".

While Americans tend to think of curry as a pungent yellow powder which seems to stain everything it comes into contact with, curry is not just a spice, but a product of a dozen or more different spices such as cumin, ginger, garlic, coriander, chili, tumeric, cardamom, cloves, nutmeg, black pepper and cinnamon; the last five being the operative elements of *garam masala*--a mixture often sprinkled on Indian entrees just before they are served. Curry also refers to any dish which is seasoned with curry powder.

Almost anything Indians make can be curried. Thus, there are meat, chicken, seafood, fish and vegetarian curries--curry in each case referring to a different combination of spices specially blended to bring out the distinctive flavor of a particular type of food. Indians usually mix the curry with one or more of a wide variety of *sambals* (condiments), many of which are *chutneys* (acid fruit condiments made with dried fruit, onions and spices) used to further draw out the flavor of the food.

While curries can be downright scrumptious, two caveats are in order. First, curries are often so nicely spiced that one tends to forget that they are, at root, a form of extremely fattening gravy. Second, when curries were originally developed there was no such thing as refrigeration, and curries were often used to mask the aroma of meat going bad. The fact that Indians tend to make a meal out of a number of small courses, rather than offering a Western-style "main course", reflects a historic acceptance of the possibility that any one course might not be altogether sound.

Some people feel that the single greatest contribution of Indian cuisine is that style of cooking known as *"tandoori"*--where meats and other items are first marinated in yogurt and spices, then broiled over charcoal in a clay oven known, predictably enough, as a "tandoor". The tandoor, however, is not an Indian invention. Rather, it was introduced to India in the 16th Century by the Mongols (hence "moghul" or "mughli" style cooking); and, to this day, is most popular in and around Delhi, where the Mongol shahs set up their provisional capital.

While tandoori cooking has come to be associated almost exclusively with chicken, virtually any type of meat, fowl or fish can be cooked in a tandoor. Indeed, when properly prepared, *"jhinga tandoori"--tandoori prawns*--is one of our favorite foods. Some restaurants serve other interesting items such as tandoori lamb chops, mixed grill or fish. A few also roast their bread in the tandoor.

Chicken curry and chicken tandoori are two of India's most popular dishes, but there are a host of other fine entrees Indians make with the bird. Chicken tikka masala, for example, is a wonderful dish which combines the two cooking styles. To create tikka masala, the chicken is first marinated, then charbroiled in a tandoor. Then it is allowed to simmer in a mild spicy (masala) sauce. *Chicken sagwala*--cooked in spinach, and *korma*--mild saffron curry, are also well worth a try.

Lamb and seafood can likewise be cooked in a tandoor or served in a curry sauce. Other popular lamb entrees include *sag gosht*--lamb cooked in a fragrant spinach sauce; *keema mattar*--minced lamb sauteed with fresh green peas; *lamb pasanda*--served in a mild sauce with almonds; and *bhuna gosht*--lamb and onions, with ginger root and a hint of garlic. Typically the only seafood offering on an Indian menu is *prawn*. You may come across an interesting Benghali dish known as *jhinga masalas*--prawn prepared in a special masala sauce, or *jhinga bhuna*--prawns in gravy.

## *Sabzi Bhandar* (Vegetarian Specialties)

Vegetarians tend to love Indian restaurants because India is one of the few major countries that doesn't treat herbivores like untouchables. Whether by design or lack of choice, many Indians are themselves vegetarians, and Indians have long known how to exalt the often overlooked vegetable into a form of *haute cuisine*. Indeed, many Indian restaurants serve as many good vegetarian dishes as meat ones; and there are even a couple in the area which do not cater to carnivores at all.

Some of India's most common non-meat offerings are *mattar paneer*--cubes of Indian farmer's cheese with green peas cooked in tomato curry; *saag (or palak) paneer*--ditto with spinach (or cheese); *aloo ghobi*--cauliflower and potatoes cooked with herbs and spices; *dal makhani*--a creamy and sometimes scrumptious lentil curry; *mushroom bhaji*--mushrooms and green peas in a mild curry sauce; *channa masala (or channa peshawari)*--garbanzo beans in a mild masala sauce; and *bengan bhartha*--eggplant stewed in tomato curry. Occasionally you may also come across *bhindi masala*--spiced okra in a mild masala sauce, but this is a seasonal dish which only rarely seems to be in season.

A word you will often see on Indian menus is *thali*. The traditional Indian *thali* is a tray full of vegetarian dishes served in small metal bowls together with raita, bread, dal, rice pilau and dessert. Although a renowned San Francisco restaurant critic recently likened the Indian thali tray to a "t.v. dinner", thalis can be quite refined, as well as filling and inexpensive.

## Side Dishes and *Rotiyaan* (Breads)

India is well respected for its tasty breads, of which there are many. The four you are most likely to be served are *paratha, poori, nan* and *chapati*. *Paratha* is a delicious but often heavily-buttered, fried whole wheat bread which is sometimes available in a "stuffed" form--the usual stuffing being *aloo* (potatoes) or meat. *Nan*, a mainstay of the North Indian diet, hails from Afghanistan, where it was originally flavored by cooking over camel dung (presumably it derives its delightful flavor from another source now). Like paratha, nan is sometimes stuffed, as in the case of *onion kulcha* and *keema nan*--minced lamb. Poori is similar to *paratha* except thinner, puffed and deep-fried. *Chapati* is an unleavened, griddle-cooked whole wheat bread.

In addition to breads, virtually all Indian restaurants serve a habit-forming side dish called *raita*. An aromatic combination of yogurt, cucumbers and spices, raita is more than a little reminiscent of Greek tzatziki. It is almost uniformly of good quality, and goes particularly well with the basmati rice *pilau (pullao, pilav)* which accompanies most Indian meals. Other common Indian side dishes are mango chutney, achaar--pickle, and a paper thin lentil wafer known as *papadum*.

### Mehakti-Hui (Beverages) and Mithaiyaan (Desserts)

In addition to the usual complement of Western drinks, many Indian restaurants also serve *mango juice, mango "shakes" and lassi*--a refreshing but, like many Indian foods, filling and fattening combination of buttermilk and yogurt. Lassi is usually plain, but is sometimes flavored with either mango or mint, and may be made either salty or sweet. Some restaurants also offer *chai*--spiced tea with milk, and/or a richer and more flavorful blend of coffee than that served at most American restaurants. A few actually brew coffee in a different way, with evaporated milk and sugar--the end-product tasting like a highly texturous cafe *au lait*. Finally, although alcoholic beverages are not an Indian specialty--the country's primary contributions on this score being a few indigenous beers--you will occasionally come across a drink called *Pimm's cup*. This is a refreshing gin sling garnished with fresh cucumber and pieces of lemon.

The same San Francisco restaurant critic who panned thali trays also recently voiced a distaste for Indian desserts. With respect, while few Indian desserts taste much like anything most Americans are used to, India boasts perhaps the most varied and interesting assortment of sweets in the world. Further, whether critically acclaimed or not, there are several Indian *namkeen* (snack) and sweet shops which make a pretty good living by serving them.

Perhaps the best Indian dessert to (so to speak) cut your teeth on is *kulfi*--rich homemade ice cream flavored with pistachios and almonds. When properly made, kulfi--sometimes called *kulfi faluda*--will have a unique crunchy texture as well as a superb taste. The worst part about kulfi is ordering it. The language barrier being what it is, about half the time you order kulfi you will get it; the other half you'll get "coffee".

Other excellent Indian desserts include *ras malai*--Indian cheese in saffron-flavored milk with nuts, mango ice cream, and *kheer*--a rich Indian rice pudding flavored with cardamom and nuts. However, the dessert you are most likely to be served is *gulab jaman*--a rose water flavored milk ball in cardamom syrup. Although we have come to like gulab jaman very much, it definitely is an acquired taste--not for everyone.

## SUE'S KITCHEN   (8/10=18)

1061 E. El Camino Real   Sunnyvale   (408) 296-6522

The odds against finding the Bay Area's best Indian cookery in a little hole in the wall in Sunnyvale might seem pretty high, but Sue's Kitchen, a relative newcomer to the Bay Area Indian restaurant scene, may well warrant this accolade. Sue's is the only Bay Area restaurant (and perhaps the only one in the nation) to specialize in the cuisine of the Southern Indian state of Andhra Pradesh, and it's a cinch you've never tasted anything quite like it before. If you are in the mood for drastic experimentation, try *uttappam*--fermented spongy pancakes ($4.75) or *avadalu*--a fritter soaked in spicy yogurt ($4.00). Another authentic South Indian appetizer Sue's offers is *masala vada*--deep-fried and spicy ground yellow lentils ($3.25). For your main course, we recommend that you pass over Sue's large selection of *dosas* and *idlis* (see introduction), and head straight for its *Malabar chicken* ($9.25). This memorable house specialty, developed for the restaurant by owner and head chef Sue Sista, is made by marinating the fowl in a special sauce for several hours, then boiling it just before it is served in the style of Kerala State. What makes the dish so tasty is the distinctive use of fresh dry-roasted spices. Also delicious, if not as innovative, is Sue's *mushroom bhaji*--sliced mushrooms in a spicy butter sauce ($8.25). Both Sue's *raita* and *basmati rice pullao*, served with every dinner, are also extremely good. Unlike some Indian restaurants which offer excellent starters but fall down when it comes time for coffee and dessert, Sue's manages to sustain a high level right through to the final course. We unreservedly recommend her South Indian Coffee ($.95) and *chai*--spiced tea ($.95), along with a plate of *ras malai* or *kulfi*--both of which are much better than the norm. Sista is not only responsible for some of the most innovative Indian recipes on any Bay Area menu, she deserves credit for the atmosphere of her restaurant too. That is because her cozy and intimate dining room is lined by lovely batiks and oils painted by Sista herself. Music and service at Sue's are also authentic. Indeed, the only disappointing thing about the restaurant--apart from its less than optimal location and some tacky duck place mats--is that it does not offer a "no smoking" section. This problem can be particularly noisome on weekends, when Sue's gets crowded. On our most recent visit, three chain-smoking masochists at the table next to ours decided to light up happy sticks just as we were about to tackle our dessert. Needless to say, somehow cancer and *kulfi* don't mix.

Hours: M-Th 11-2, 5-9; F 11-2, 5-10; Sa 5-10, Su 5-9.
Cards: MC/V.

## GAYLORD INDIA (9/9=18)

900 North Point (Ghirardelli Square)   San Francisco   771-8822

Generally speaking, we don't gravitate towards a city's most popular and expensive ethnic restaurants because, in an effort to accommodate the American aesthetic and palate, such establishments tend to sacrifice a bit of their native charm. Gaylord India is a pleasant exception. Here's a restaurant (a chain actually, with locations all over the world in such chic places as London, Hong Kong and Beverly Hills) which has not let unparalleled success go to its collective head. The atmosphere at (most) every Gaylord's is individual, authentic and attractive. Similarly, for a multi-branch operation, Gaylord's service is remarkably pleasant. Most importantly, perhaps, as most Indian food lovers know, Gaylord's cuisine is in a class (almost) by itself. One of the things that makes Gaylord's special is that, despite the restaurants' exalted status, it doesn't attempt to do too much, and it doesn't go in for anything too modish. The restaurant's appetizers and breads, for example, are basically the same items you'd find at any "regular" Indian restaurant. They just taste better. Likewise, Gaylord's tandoori and vegetable selections are pretty similar to what you'd expect to find elsewhere--but they are outstanding. Indeed, if you've somehow avoided the pleasure of sampling tandoori cuisine before, this is probably the best place in the Bay Area to try it. With the exception of Gaylord's Cafe (in Newark), all of the local Gaylord's feature similar menus. They vary a great deal, however, in ambience. In this respect, Gaylord's Ghirardelli is probably the most outstanding. In addition to hand-carved wooden statues, a brick and glass tandoor, live plants, and pillows--lots of pillows--Gaylord's Ghirardelli boasts one of San Francisco's finest bay views and live kathak dance performances during its extremely popular Sunday brunch ($13.95 per person for a high-quality multi-course buffet). Although the main emphasis of Gaylord's Ghirardelli, as with other Gaylord's, will remain on fine tandoori-style cooking, owner Kishore Kripalani advises that the restaurant is soon to introduce regional dishes from different parts of India. With dinner entrees averaging $12.00--$15.00, Gaylord's is a little pricy; but you definitely get what you pay for. Reservations advised.

Hours: M-Sa-12-2, 5-11. Sunday buffet: 12(n)-3.
Cards: All. Personal checks accepted.

## INDIAN CAFE (THE)   (10/7=17)

1810 University Ave.  Berkeley  548-4110

For a representative of the Indian subcontinent to survive and flourish in the Bay Area's competitive Indian restaurant market, it has to offer something out of the ordinary. Berkeley's Indian Cafe--an offbeat and charming place located in a loft at the back of an Indian spice and sundry shop--does just that. Indeed, before you even get to the loft it is necessary to travel down rows crammed with spices, condiments, bedspreads and the like, then ascend a stairway adorned with pictures of typical Indian scenes. So, by the time you arrive at the your table, you are already well on your way to feeling "transported." In the tastefully decorated Cafe itself there may be more colorful hand-painted Indian cloths than in any room of comparable size in Northern California. To sit anywhere in such a room is a pleasure, but we suggest taking a table near the front which affords the chance to do some pleasant "window shopping" while you dine. While the food at the Cafe has not always been of the highest quality, we have noticed a decided upturn in the past few years. For example, its tangy *raita*--an Indian yogurt and dill equivalent of Greek *tzatziki* ($1.25) is now to be counted among the Bay Area's best; and several of its entrees, especially vegetarian offerings like *mushroom curry* ($5.50) and *sag paneer* ($6.00), are excellent. Connoisseurs of Indian desserts also have a treat in store. The Cafe's *mango custard* ($1.25) is one of the premier Indian desserts around and its mango shake with ground nuts ($1.50) is almost as good. In any case, when one considers the Cafe's inconceivably low prices it's hard to be hypercritical. *Prawns vindaloo*--a spicy saute of prawns and onions in a mild, flavorful coconut sauce is, at $8.50, the restaurant's most expensive a la carte dish. Its most expensive dinner for two (which no two people we know could finish), costs a mere $25.00. While in this book we make every effort to be "price blind"--judging a restaurant's ambience and cuisine without regard to cost--it seems a bit unfair to measure the culinary merits of a bargain-priced place like the Indian Cafe against those of restaurants which charge substantially more. Admittedly, the Indian Cafe may not boast the glitter of Gaylord's, the urbane sophistication of Bombay Palace or the world class culinary magic of the peninsula's vastly underrated Sue's Kitchen. However, having plunked down all of $20.00 for a meal that could easily have cost twice that and still been worth it, we think the Indian Cafe deserves to rank right up there with the Bay Area's all around best.

Hours: M-Sa 11:30-3:30, 5:30-9.
Cards: All major.

## CAFE BOMBAY (8/9=17)

400 Valley Way   Milpitas   (408) 263-1061

Milpitas may not be one of the world's great bastions of ethnic culture but, smack dab in the middle of a Best Western hotel, there is a restaurant threatening to change all that. Don't get us wrong. Cafe Bombay does not have the almost mystical atmosphere of an India House--it boasts no camel-gut lamps or hand-painted chairs--but it does offer a peaceful, almost meditative Indian atmosphere which is impressive without being ostentatious or even, for that matter, all that out of the ordinary. Somehow, these same attributes are inculcated into Cafe Bombay's food itself. Its specialty of the house is tandoori-style cooking and few Bay Area restaurants do it better. The restaurant's *tandoori chicken*--marinated in yogurt with saffron, ginger and garlic ($5.95--"half", $9.00--"full") is a real delight. Although there is not much unique on the Cafe Bombay menu, *Kabuli naan* ($2.00)--a type of bread indigenous to Afghanistan and the "Northwest frontier" which is stuffed with ground almonds or cashews, spices and even a few dried fruits--is a relative rarity. It is thoroughly enjoyable and not to be missed. Another out of the ordinary dish is *pachrang biryani*--basmati rice cooked with mixed vegetables and covered with cheese ($5.95). Some more familiar items, like "chicken saagwala" and "keema mattar (both $5.95), are particularly good here, as are Cafe Bombay's renderings of *dal makhani* and *sabzi masala* (which you'll recognize elsewhere as "vegetable korma"--both $4.25). Cafe Bombay's vegetarian ($7.95) and non-vegetarian ($9.95) thalis are excellent values but, if you are in the mood for a *real* feast, go for the *shahi dastarkhwan*--royal spread. Basically, you'll get everything that comes with both thalis, along with a tandoori mixed grill, *papad* and chutney ($29.95 for two). You won't be able to finish it all. So, we recommend that you get a doggy bag for your entrees and save some room for Cafe Bombay's rich "ras malai" ($2.50), which is better than both its kulfi ($2.00) and *kheer* ($1.50). Although Cafe Bombay serves a quality luncheon buffet (for $5.95) every weekday (and a special champagne brunch on Sunday--$7.95), you'll definitely want to pass on breakfast. While the Cafe does *serve* breakfast (indeed, it may be the only Indian restaurant in the Bay Area to do so), there is nothing on its breakfast menu which even remotely resembles an Indian dish--an accommodation to the hotel patrons who, no doubt, would not take well to being served *pakoras* instead of pancakes.

Hours: Daily 10-10.
Cards: All major.

## GANGES (THE)   (8/8=16)

775 Frederick St.   San Francisco   661-7290

Unsurreptitiously located on a quiet street in a residential neighborhood, the Ganges is not a place you'd be apt to discover during a casual stroll. In fact, it isn't all that easy to find even when you know where it is. But once you've arrived, you'll quickly realize that you've happened upon a special place. First, of the 60 plus Bay Area Indian restaurants, the Ganges is the only one which specializes in the cuisine of Gujarat State (just north of Bombay), and it is one of the few that offers a strictly vegetarian menu (not even gelatin or eggs are served.) In addition, the Ganges is one of the Bay Area's most inexpensive places to hear live sitar music (Thursday through Saturday night.) But perhaps the most outstanding thing about the Ganges is its invitation to customers to advise the kitchen of any dietary restrictions they might have. You won't find too many restaurants asking you to make their life difficult so yours can be more healthful. The Ganges is divided into two sections, one with "regular" tables and chairs and the other with low tables and pillows. If you are physically fit, we'd suggest you call ahead and reserve the pillows. Although situated farther away from the music they are more fun, especially because the small restaurant is tilted at an angle which requires whomever is sitting on the outside of the table to strain to avoid sliding. Although the ambience at The Ganges is good, its food is better; and the menu features a whole host of dishes offered nowhere else. Such unfamiliar items as *shak dhoku*--dumplings in beans, *shak muthia*--spinach kababs in beans, *panchkutiu curry*--sweet and sour vegetables and *lindhiu*--stuffed vegetables with lima beans, are just the type of innovative finds that temporarily-grounded world travellers dream about. The Ganges' menu alternates between these and more familiar dishes like *chana masala* and *mattar paneer*, so not all entrees will be available at any given time. There will also be some innovative daily specials such as *stuffed banana*. While the absence of meat and fowl is not a big selling point to some, the diversity and extraordinary quality of the Ganges' entrees is bound to put a hurt on even the most carnivorous appetite. You'll definitely also want to try one of Ganges' desserts because, like the entrees, these are far from ordinary. *Ladu*, for example, is a delicious garbanzo flour concoction spiced with cardamom which is rarely available except at a few Indian sweet shops. *Sheera*--a farina-based dessert with cinnamon, is even less common (both $1.25).

Hours: M-Sa 5-9:30.
Cards: All major.

## BOMBAY PALACE (6/10=16)

2801 Leavenworth Ave. (The Cannery) San Francisco 776-3666

Although we view this book as being, first and foremost, a travel guide, we recognize that the main interest of many who read it is to find restaurants which serve great food, regardless of what they look and feel like. Have we got a place for you! Though the San Francisco branch of what has become a world-wide chain is set in a former cannery, the atmosphere at Bombay Palace is nothing to write home about. It's fancy, it's fine, but it's not very authentic; with virtually no Indian paraphernalia and only a smattering of little prints which you have to walk up to before you can tell they are Indian. Once you get over the disappointment of realizing that somebody took the Bombay out of Bombay Palace, however, you can have a pretty good time. Unlike most Indian restaurants which specialize in the cuisine of a single region, the Palace guard has combed the Indian subcontinent to come up with a variety of superb dishes you will find nowhere else. Offered are appetizers such as *crab goa*--crab flakes sauted with onion, coconut and tomatoes ($6.25) and *patra ni machi*--fish filet with hot mint chutney, steamed in a banana leaf ($5.25); and entrees like *sali boti*--lamb cubes stewed with dried apricots (a dish from the subcontinent's Northwest Frotier--$11.55); *gosht patiala*--lamb cooked with ginger, garlic and garam masala (from Patiala State--$11.55); and Bombay's own *noorani kebab*--fillets of tandoori chicken breast marinated in cashew paste with fresh herbs ($9.55). In addition, one of the best vegetarian dishes we've ever had is the Palace's *paneer mutter makhani*--homemade cottage cheese cooked in a rich sauce with cashews and garden peas ($6.55), and its *navratna biryani*--basmati rice with garden vegetables ($6.55) is also worth a try. If you are a gourmet on a budget, try paying a visit to the Palace on Sunday for brunch between 11:00 and 2:00. No accommodation to Western tastes here--the brunch menu is all Indian (except for the champagne) and this is one of the best Indian buffets around (much better, for example, then the lunch buffet served at Gaylord's Embarcadero). Imagine: unlimited access to astoundingly good renditions of *tandoori chicken, chicken tikka, vegetable jal fraize, dal maharani, basmati rice, naan, raita* and *bengan bharta* for only $9.95 including champagne. This is one of the best values in Indian dining around.

Hours: S-Th 11:30-2:30, 5-10; F-Sa 5-10:30.
Cards: All major.

## MAHARAJA (8/8=16)

528 San Mateo Ave.  San Bruno  871-5566

Maharaja's music is nice and its service is above average, but what really accounts for its high rating is the homey feeling it exudes that is not present at most other Bay Area Indian restaurants. Then there is the delicious smoky aroma emanating from its tandoor which you can smell all the way from your car. (Do we like the Maharaja because it subconsciously reminds us of a long forgotten visit to a Rawalpindi bazaar?) Whatever the subliminal reasons, we like Maharaja a lot. Unlike many Indian restaurants, Maharaja's food tends not to be unduly heavy or greasy. A case in point is its *channa masala*--chickpea curry, which is totally unlike versions we have sampled at inferior restaurants. The beans are whole and dry, not mushed into a spicy curry sauce which, however good it might be, is guaranteed to add about 1,000 calories to your frame. Maharaja also offers 4 lunch specials: vegetable ($4.50), chicken ($5.50), lamb ($5.95) and barbecue ($5.95). All come with *Lahori naan*--a crisp white flour bread baked in the tandoor ($1.00), as well as basmati rice and a mixed vegetable entree. As you may have gathered when we mentioned the smoke, Maharaja's barbecue combination is a must. In addition to the above, it comes with a very tasty *seekh kabab* and one of the most expertly prepared pieces of *tandoori chicken* around. Dinners are considerably more expensive, but still a good value. All entrees can be ordered either as complete dinners (with rice, bread, *papad* and chutney) or a la carte for $2.00 less. (Prices listed in this review are for complete dinners.) In addition to traditional North Indian fare, Maharaja offers quite a few Pakistani dishes. In addition to Lahori Naan and *Lahori Kheer*--a cold dessert of milk pudding with dried fruits--Maharaja serves a Peshawari dish known as *chicken johl fraizee*--pieces of chicken with tomatoes, onions, peppers, garlic and ginger. Also available is *nawabi murg tikka*--boneless chicken marinated in tandoori masala then charbroiled ($10.95)--a specialty of the North Indian city of Lacknow. But perhaps Maharaja's greatest achievement is its *tandoori lamb*--tender pieces of lamb leg marinated with spiced yogurt, then cooked over a slow heat in the style of India's Northwest Frontier ($11.95). If you are in the mood to try something vegetarian that's a little out of the ordinary, your best bet is a puree of fresh spinach with potatoes and spices known as *aloo palak* ($6.50). The barbecued foods are really your best choice, but either way you won't go home unhappy.

Hours: M-Sa 11-2; Daily 5-10.
Cards: All major.

## NORTH INDIA (7/9=16)

3131 Webster St.  San Francisco  931-1556

North India has some atmosphere, but not as much as a hole in the wall this far from the financial district ought to have. Its antique velvet chairs and pink tablecloths, overlooked by drawings of foot soldiers from a bygone colonial era, are nice but don't seem particularly appropriate. There are also a few large brass urns and the like strewn about, but nothing really special. Like many restaurants that emphasize food almost to the exclusion of atmosphere, North India's menu is more extensive than is perhaps necessary or realistic. Its dinner menu alone features nine chicken dishes, nine tandoori dishes, and eleven types of bread; and North India's lunch menu is offered *in addition to*, rather than in lieu of, its dinner menu. Thus the menu (which starts off "God Bless America" and proceeds through a gratuitous history of the owner's life) manifests the view that Americans cannot be content unless they are given the option of having it all. Delightful mixed appetizers and a wonderful lightly seasoned lentil soup give way to several mediocre and overpriced entrees like *seafood tandoori* ($9.95 for lunch, a hefty $18.95 otherwise), as well as some admirable ones like *dahi bhalla*--white lentil dumplings in lightly seasoned yogurt and tamarind sauce served cold with raisins and green onions ($6.25); *shrimp chat*--cold shrimp with diced potatoes, vegetables and fresh lemon ($7.95); *chicken daraiwala*--cooked with fresh garlic and ginger in a semi-dry sauce, served in an Indian "wok" ($14.95); and *karai gosht*--lamb cubes cooked in the same manner as *chicken daraiwala*, also served wok-style ($15.95). The most unusual items on North India's menu, however, are *Bombay pakoras*--calamari dipped in chick-pea batter and fried with onions and spinach ($7.95). The overall impression of North India is that it is above average--good but inconsistent--and not nearly as good as it *could* be. Although many of its dishes are superb, one can't help feeling that an out of the way place that commands dinner prices ranging from $12.95 to $18.95 (not including beverage or dessert) had *better* be good. In 1988, Zagat's rated North India as San Francisco's premier Indian restaurant which, from the standpoint of cuisine alone, on any given day it might rise to be. However, as a total package, North India is far too inconsistent to rank up there with the great ones. Considering the restaurant's decided lack of ambience, you can do better for the price.

Hours: M-F 11:30-2:30, 5-11, Sa 5-11, Su 5-10.
Cards: All.

## GAYLORD INDIA   7/9=16

317 Stanford Shopping Center   Palo Alto   (326-8761)

Though most Gaylords are good, and even though the Ghirardelli Square location--with its outstanding Bay view and popular Sunday brunch--gets the bulk of the press, it is the Gaylord in Stanford shopping center we like best. The restaurant is pretty and authentic, with gorgeous Indian paintings and superb service. Indeed, for a shopping center location, the ambience at Gaylord's Palo Alto is almost too good to be true. It may also have the best food of any local Gaylords. Its *navratan korma*--mixed vegetables in a mild cream sauce, is the best we have tasted anywhere, and two other dishes: *dal makhani*--creamed lentils in spices, and *chicken pasanda*--boneless chicken chunks in a mildly spiced cream sauce, are in a class by themselves. An unusual Gaylord offering is *nargisi kofta*--minced lamb meat balls stuffed with eggs in gravy. If you are looking for a nice place to relax after doing some serious shopping, you won't find a much better place than this.

Hours: Daily--12-2:30, 5-10.
Cards: All major.

## INDIA HOUSE   (10/6=16)

350 Jackson St.   San Francisco   392-0744

India House, a Bay Area fixture since 1947, is the oldest Indian restaurant, not only in San Francisco, but in all of North America. A single visit will explain its longevity. From its ornate king's chairs right down to the genuine bronze sugar bowls which grace every table, as far as ambience, this place has it all. Moreover, with peaceful music and its staff's unhurried manner, India House, in spite of its downtown location, always seems so serene that you may arrive in a "type A" mood, yet exit feeling peaceful as a monk. One tends to be so grateful for any kind of ethnic restaurant in the Financial District that quality of cuisine seems like an afterthought. Indeed, considering that meals at India House do not come cheap, they are not as good as they should be. Among its most innovative offerings are *bermuda creamed chicken* with sherry ($13.75), *egg curry* (11.50), and *Bombay duck*--sun-dried fish sticks ($2.00). It also serves a potent *Pimm's cup*--gin and cucumber in a pewter goblet.

Hours: M-F 11:30-2, 5:30-10:30; Sa 5:30-10:30.
Cards: All.

## SABINA (8/8=16)

1628 Webster St. Oakland 268-0170

Sabina's lovely atmosphere is primarily attributable to the extraordinary building in which it is housed. A one time tile showroom, Sabina has one of the loveliest facades of any Bay Area restaurant. Inside, a brick floor, curving blue-tile staircase and inlaid tile fountain, make the dining room one you'll not only enjoying eating in, but would kill to have in your home. A tasteful arrangement of traditional paintings, beads and other Indian embellishments enhances Sabina's already spectacular atmsophere. While the food at Sabina would not have to be very special to warrant a special trip, it is. Sabina offers a superb "eleven course" lunch buffet ($4.95). Five of the courses are bread, rice, chutney, tea and coffee, but who cares? You could live for a week on the other six--one of which, *chicken makwani*, is splendid. Don't come expecting to be overwhelmed by feelings of welcome, however; management is somewhat aloof. Still, with all Sabina has going for it, you could pay a lot more to do worse.

Hours: M-F 11:30-3, 5:30-9:30; Sa-Su 5:30-9:30.
Cards: All major.

## INDIA PALACE (7/7=14)

707 Redwood Hwy. Mill Valley 388-3350

About the last thing an unsuspecting visitor would expect to find at a Route 101 Travelodge is an Indian restaurant with a hand-painted mural the length of its outside wall. The mural tells you that you've made it to the India Palace, an unlikely gem in the rough in Marin County. Inside, a glittering incarnation of Ganesh, Indian's elephant-God, reigns supreme over an attractively-appointed interior. However, while the Palace's food is quite palatable, there are no surprises, and we have yet to be served a truly outstanding meal. Your best bet is *shahi khorma*--lamb cubes with almonds ($10.95), although we also like its spicy *bengan bharta* ($7.95)--a house specialty. Two thumbs down on its *saag paneer*, mixed appetizer plate ($6.95) and *keema nan* (sparingly stuffed with minced lamb--$3.00). Also, considering that except for two somewhat overpriced "royal feasts" ($18.95 and $19.95) dinners don't come with a thing, prices at India Palace are no bargain.

Hours: M 5:30-10; Tu-Sa 11:30-2, 5:30-10; Su 12(n)-2, 5:30-10.
Cards: All Major.

## PEACOCK (THE)   (5/9=14)

2800 Van Ness Ave.   San Francisco   928-7001

Attractively located in a 1906 Victorian mansion once belonging to Barry Goldwater Jr., the Peacock is certainly one of the more impressive-looking Indian restaurants in the Bay Area; and its cuisine is virtually without peer. Lamentably, the restaurant's ambience, while pleasant, is not at all Indian. Indeed, while its main dining room is graced by such ornate items as a tiled fireplace and antique velvet chairs, it contains not one solitary subcontinental knickknack. When the music of the day happens to be classical, as it was on our last visit, you might as well sup at a Wine Country Inn. What makes the dearth of genuine Indian atmosphere regrettable is that the Peacock's cuisine is so undeniably good. Try one of the Peacock's lunch "combinations", particularly *palak paneer* and *bangan bharta*--broiled eggplant with peas and spices--one of the most satisfying vegetarian dishes around. At $6.50, this combination may qualify for the sale of the century, too.

Hours: Su-Th 11:30-2, 5:30-10; F 11:30-2, 5:30-10:30; Sa  5:30-10:30.
Cards: All. No personal checks.

## ROYAL INDIA   (6/7=13)

1400 Franklin St.  Oakland  268-9000

Usually it is a cardinal mistake to order a buffet because warmed-over mass-produced food will rarely be reflective of the best a restaurant has to offer. Although this is undoubtedly the case at Royal India too, we were surprised to find that many of its buffet items--such as *raita* and *kheer*--surpass some individually prepared dishes we've had at other comparably-priced places, and its *dal makhani* is exceptional. Plus, its entire multi-course buffet is offered daily for only $5.50. If 11 courses aren't enough, come on Saturday and try the *17* course variety ($11.50)--designed to take you, literally, from soup to nuts, then leave you waddling. Royal India's atmosphere doesn't quite measure up to its food. While pleasant enough--its music is nice and there are a few Indian artifacts--the primary focus is on an incongruous set of steerhorns which somehow managed to survive the transition from what used to be The Old Steakhouse. Truly ironic, since no beef is served.

Hours: M-F 11:30-2, 5:30-9:30; Sa 5:30-9:30; Su 11:30-2:30.
Cards: All major.

## INDIA KASHMIR (7/6=13)

1888 Solano Ave. Berkeley 525-1122

As you pass through the exquisite hand-carved doors at India Kashmir you are greeted by a huge bronze statue and a solitary camel-gut lamp. Inside, the restaurant features an intimate atmosphere apparently geared more to the tastes of North Berkeley's affluent young than to serious Indian culture vultures bent on an authentic Eastern experience. Since the food at India Kashmir is likewise prepared with the neophyte in mind, it is a good place to take somebody who is unfamiliar with, but eager to sample, India cuisine. Indeed, one of its curry dishes, *chicken shurva*, is so mild that the menu touts it as a good way to be "introduced to the joys of Indian cuisine" ($8.25 with condiments and steamed rice, $11.50 as a complete dinner). One of the pleasant surprises at India Kashmir is its "soup kashmiri"--a delightful yellow split pea soup which provides a pleasant respite from the usual *dal*. Other finds are *curried chollay*-- garbanzo bean ($8.95) and *lamb kashmiri* ($12.50).

Hours: Daily 5:30-9:30.
Cards: All major.

## PASAND MADRAS CUISINE (7/6=13)

802 B St. San Rafael 456-6099

Since opening its initial "branch" in Emeryville in 1975, Pasand has added four locations--each of which seems to suffer from chain mentality. San Rafael is probably Pasand's best location, with pretty gewgaws and above average service. But even here the food is not as good as you'd expect from a place that has not only survived the tough Bay Area Indian restaurant competition, but has gone forth and multiplied (four Northern California locations, as well as one in Yonkers, New York which Pasand has inexplicably been advertising as "opening soon" for the past several years). Despite the existence of several competitors--all of which serve comparable or superior South Indian food--Pasand's unaccountably continues to tout itself as "the only restaurant in the Bay Area serving authentic South Indian Cuisine". It also boasts "very affordable prices", which is debatable, given that portions are not extraordinary and its dinners offer no choice at all about such things as bread, soup or dessert.

Hours: M-F 11:30-3, 5-10; Sa-Su 11:30-10.
Cards: All major.

## GITA'S   (5/8=13)

1048 Market St.   San Francisco   864-4306

This is a would-be top ten restaurant with middle ten atmosphere in a bottom ten location. Although its music is okay and there are a few sparsely placed wall hangings, you have to close your eyes (and open your mouth) to imagine that you are really in India. Few menu items are unique, but what Gita does serve is excellent; and several of Gita's creations, including *patra*--steamed spicy taro leaves ($2.50), are better than anywhere else in the city. Also of special interest are Gita's *potato bonda*--four mashed potato and chili patties dipped in a seasoned batter ($2.50), and its excellent *chana masala*. For $3.95, you can't do much better anywhere in the Bay Area. Gita's also features a full complement of South Indian dishes, including a plethora of *dosas*--Indian crepes made from a mixture of Indian grains and flour. While these are filling and hearty, they are definitely an acquired taste.

Hours: M-Th 11-3:30, 4:30-8; F-Sa-11-9.
Cards: No. Checks accepted.

## PASAND MADRAS CUISINE   (7/6=13)

3701 El Camino Rl.   Santa Clara   (408) 241-5150}

Probably the best atmosphere of the four Pasands, despite its heart of shopping center location; still, the food at this Pasand is not as good as one would hope. Some of the best items on its menu are its superb raita, made with fresh cucumbers, and its extensive alcoholic beverage list, which features *Pimm's cup* and a few other specialty drinks you're not likely to find at your local bar. Two of Pasand's better non-alcoholic beverage items are "Madras special coffee" (brewed with milk--$.75) and mango juice ($1.25).

Hours: Daily 11:30-10.
Cards: All major.

## TAJ KESRI (5/8=13)

12221 San Pablo Ave. (Mira Vista Plaza) Richmond 233-3817

Like anyone else, we are subject to predispositions. Before our first visit to Taj Kesri we happened to see an advertisement indicating that a respected Bay Area critic had proclaimed the Taj to be the "best Indian restaurant in the Bay Area". Our expectations going in, therefore, were rather high. While the food at Taj is good, in order to think that this is one of the Bay Area's *best* Indian restaurants, you'd have to be oblivious to a number of its pronounced limitations. For one thing, if you replaced the Taj's few painted cloths with sombreros, the restaurant could be converted into a Mexican tortilleria in about 10 minutes--nothing else about the Taj giving even the remotest hint of India. Likewise, while the Taj has a stereo, we managed to get through an entire meal without hearing any Indian sounds; and the feel of the restaurant is far from festive. Foodwise, the Taj's vegetable *pakoras* ($2.00) are tasty and non-greasy, while its *navrattan korma* ($5.50) is rich but delicious.

Hours: M-F 11-2:30, 5-10; Sa 5-10; Su 11:30-2, 5-10.
Cards: All major. No checks.

## AROOJ (7/5=12)

2371 Contra Costa Blvd. Pleasant Hill 934-7740

Arooj is an unpretentious little place located in a mini-mall just off highway 680. Gold and silver-plated trays adorn its walls, while the windows are covered with gauche Madras drapes; and a studded batik of a Raja and his servants covers an always-empty dessert case. The Mexican feel of the place (did Arooj used to be a Mexican restaurant?) is enhanced by the uncharacteristic use of plastic table cloths and tortilla trays in which crunchy, doughy *roti* is served. Since Arooj is at root Pakistani, not India--and since most Pakistanis are Muslim, not Hindu--at Arooj you are apt to discover something you may never have seen on a subcontinental menu before: beef. Try *chapli kabab*--spiced ground beef, onion, tomato and hot pepper ($1.60), or Arooj's unusual meat entree *nihari*--boneless beef in herbs and spices served with fresh ginger (5.25). The service at Arooj is attentive, and the restaurant offers good value, especially at lunch when it features three curry specials for under $5.00.

Hours: Daily 11-10.
Cards: All major. Checks accepted.

## BOMBAY CUISINE (6/6=12)

2006 Ninth St.  Berkeley  843-9601

The first things you notice at Bombay Cuisine are its tasteful wall hangings which, although poorly lit, are interesting enough to keep the eye engaged. The restaurant offers a fairly typical assortment of dishes which are adequate but generally forgettable. Its *papad*, for example, are tasteless; especially since they are served without tamarack or mint; the peas in its *mattar panir* taste like "Birdseyes", and its *prawn tikka* appetizer is really a "shrimp" tikka appetizer--not worth its entree-like price ($5.95). There are a couple of fairly uncommon appetizers on the Bombay Cuisine menu, however: *khaman dhokla*--steamed chickpeas ($2.50) and *patra*--steamed taro leaves ($2.50). The restaurant's other novel item is *badam-pista-nu-dudh* ($2.00)--a warm, appealing liquid version of kulfi. Also good is Cuisine's "*gajar* (carrot) *halwah*" which has the consistency of pumpkin pie and tastes nothing like either carrots or halvah. A can't miss is Bombay Cuisine's Indian-style coffee ($1.50).

Hours: Tu-Su 11:30-3, 5-9.
Cards: All major.

## HIMALAYA (6/6=12)

12471 San Pablo Ave.  Richmond  236-4148

High ceiling fans and simple Indian ornaments provide an authentic breath of North India; and the restaurant's family-run feel allows you to fantasize that you are visiting someone abroad. Unfortunately, while you do feel like you're in India when you're at Himalaya, you don't necessarily feel like you're glad you came. It's hard to put your finger on what's wrong. Its food is good enough, if not unworldly; and its atmosphere is as authentic as that at some restaurants we've rated higher. Possibly its the 1950's diner feeling which does the place in; or the restaurant's depressing location. Or maybe it's because a family-like atmosphere is only a plus when the family seems happy to see you. While there is nothing unique on Himalaya's menu, there are no unpleasant surprises either; and both its vegetarian and non-vegetarian thalis are good values ($8.99 and $9.99). Best dish: *aloo gobi*--curried cauliflower and potatoes. The restaurant also serves a variety of reasonably priced sweets.

Hours: Daily 11-10.
Cards: AE. Checks okay.

## SAYEED KABABS   (6/6=12)

1562 Halford Ave.   Santa Clara   (408) 985-6767

Its walls are bare, its tables are empty, and its plastic overhead menu is right out of a school cafeteria but, despite evident drawbacks, there is something authentic and appealing about Sayeed's. Extremely pleasant service and music is part of the attraction. *Kababs* (*seekh, shish* and others) are another part. But our favorite things about Sayeed's are its novel desserts such as *falooda*, which tastes something like a vanilla noodle milkshake ($1.50). Also try Sayeed's *shahi tukre*.

Hours: Daily 11-9.
Cards: No.

## GAYLORD'S   (5/7=12)

One Embarcadero Center   San Francisco   397-7775

Of all Bay Area Gaylords, the Embarcadero location probably leaves the most to be desired. While its menu is similar to those of other Gaylords, in other respects it is a cut below. Its food isn't bad and its multi-course lunch buffet is reasonable ($9.95), but service is a bit impersonal and the restaurant charges high prices for nothing particularly out of the ordinary.

Hours: Daily 11:30-2:30, 5-10.
Cards: All major.

## INDIA PAVILLION   (5/7=12)

2914 College Ave.   Berkeley   841-6871

The problem with India Pavillion is not its decor, which is lovely, or its food, which is good. Rather, as with Taj Kesri, which is under the same management, India Pavillion's problems seem to stem from a lack of genuine warmth. The Pavillion does boast a couple of fine tandoori items you won't find in too many other places such as trout ($9.95) and game hen, as well as a delicious *chicken palak*--with spinach ($8.75).

Hours: M-Th 11-10; F-Sa 11-10:30.
Cards: V/MC. Accepts personal checks.

## NEW DELHI JUNCTION (5/6=11)

2556 Telegraph Ave.  Berkeley  486-0477

New Delhi Junction, which replaced the delightful Mount Everest last year, got off to a fast start, garnering some very favorable reviews. However, while clean and pleasant, New Delhi's decor is nothing special, and there are few surprises on its menu. So, when its regular items aren't done extremely well, there isn't much reason to seek New Delhi Junction out in its hard to find South Berkeley mini-mall location. On our last visit, we spent $30.00 for a nothing special lunch, indifferently served.

Hours: Tu-Su 11:30-2, 5:30-9.
Cards: All major.

## MOTHER INDIA (6/5=11)

1459 University Ave.  Berkeley  486-8268

One of the newest products of Berkeley's Indian restaurant boom, Mother India is attractive, with some nice decorations including what is probably the Bay Area's most imposing map of India. Service is extremely attentive, to the point of being too deferential, and Mother India offers some pretty good specialty items, including a couple you won't see on many local Indian restaurant menus, such as *coconut soup* ($1.95).

Hours: Daily 11-10 (exc. F-Sa until 10:30).
Cards: V/MC. Personal checks accepted.

## PASAND MADRAS CUISINE (5/6=11)

2286 Shattuck Ave.  Berkeley  549-2559

Instead of the beautiful batiks which grace other Indian establishments, the first picture you'll notice at Berkeley's Pasand is a large portrait of a horse (which looks as though it may have been a self-portrait). There is little else about Pasand to distinguish it as being Indian. What saves it are above average South Indian food and live musical performances which, fortunately, unlike with Pasand in San Francisco, are Indian.

Hours: Daily 11:30-10.
Cards: All Major. Personal checks accepted.

## GAYLORD INDIA CAFE  (4/6=10)

3900 New Park Mall  Newark  796-4305

If you want a complete Indian experience, you will have to travel elsewhere; but if all you crave is a snack, Gaylord's Newark is the place to be. Why the world's foremost Indian restaurant chain would open a cafe in a Newark shopping center beats us. But once you overcome the shock of discovering a Gaylord's heart in a Wendy's body, you will quickly be impressed by the Cafe's astonishing diversity of snacks and sweets, from *carrot halwah* to *white pumpkin pethas*.

Hours: Daily-11-10.
Cards: All major.

## BOMBAY EXPRESS  (4/6=10)

32 Valencia St.  San Francisco  621-7226

This restaurant's facade is so uninviting you wonder what would motivate someone who wasn't doing a review to go in. Inside is only a little more pleasant, with tasteful subcontinental wall hangings clashing mercilessly with an unspeakable psychedelic clock which sends rays of weirdness out over the room. But B.E.'s prices are excellent and its food is good. Try *patra* ($2.50) and *mattar bharata*--pea and eggplant curry.

Hours: Tu-Su 11-9.
Cards: V/MC.

## MAHARANI  (n/r)

1025 University Ave.  Berkeley  848-7777

Maharani touts itself as the Bay Area's first "fast food" Indian restaurant. This isn't true for two reasons. It wasn't the "first" Indian fast food restaurant, and it's not particularly fast. Further, while Maharani has virtually no Indian atmosphere and service is, at best, marginal, its prices aren't cheap. Perhaps the best thing about Maharani is that it offers a couple of dinners designed to be low in calories, sodium and cholesterol.

Hours: Su-Th 11-8, F-Sa 11-9.
Cards: All major.

## ANNALAKSHMI (n/r)

24 Sixth St. San Francisco 553-8184

Outside looks more like Bombay than one might like; but inside, Anna's is clean and comfortable, with friendly service and some tasty items at dirt cheap prices. Advice to owners: nix the pasta.

Hours: M-Sa 11-8.
Cards: No. Personal checks accepted.

## SUJATHA'S (n/r)

1584 Halford Ave. Santa Clara (408) 984-5280)

The original Sujatha's (there's a bigger one in Berkeley) hasn't got much atmosphere, but it does offer some decent desserts like *pumpkin petha* and *cashew burfi* ($5.99--$6.99 lb.), and its okay for takeout.

Hours: Daily 11-9.
Cards: All major.

## SHAIKH'S INDIA FOODS (n/r)

393 California Ave. Palo Alto 327-6555

Its tables & chairs look like they were filched from a school cafeteria, and its dispose-it-yourself receptacles remind one of dining at Arby's; but this unpretentious place serves up decent food at obscenely low prices.

Hours: M-F 11-2, 4:30-7; Sa 11:30-2:30.
Cards: None. Checks accepted.

## INDIA GARDEN (n/r)

120 Hazelwood Dr. South San Francisco 952-8487

India Garden, formerly known as "Heavenly Restaurant", and before that as "Nirvana", has the distinction of having been misnamed 3 times.

Hours: Tu-Th 5-10; F-Su 5-10:30.
Cards: All major.

## PASAND MADRAS CUISINE (n/r)

1875 Union St. San Francisco 922-4498

When we dine at an Indian restaurant, we'd rather listen to a nice tape of Ali Akbar Khan or even waves crashing on a seashore than a live "blues" performance. The other Pasands are better.

Hours: Daily 11:30-10, cabaret until 2 a.m.
Cards: All major.

## BOMBAYWALA (n/r)

421 Alma St. Palo Alto 323-1195

B'wala looks more like a frozen yogurt shop than an Indian restaurant, but prices are right and its food is innovative, if not particularly exciting. Ever try a cheddar omelette with *chapati* and *raita*?

Hours: Daily 7:30(a)-10(p).
Cards: No.

## TANDORI (n/r)

267 Shoreline Blvd. Mill Valley 388-8646

Somewhat quaint but small, crowded and lugubriously slow. Two of our orders were forgotten entirely. Tandori's *simla mirch*--tandoori bell pepper stuffed with mixed vegetables ($4.95) is worth a try--if it comes.

Hours: Daily 11:30-10.
Cards: None. Accepts personal checks.

## GOVINDA'S (n/r)

86 Carl St. San Francisco 753-9073

A bit, not much, Indian atmosphere and a couple of "Indian" dishes (*Indian fettucini*, yum.). Steer clear of the halvah.

Hours: M-Sa 11:30-9.
Cards: No. Personal checks accepted.

## SUJATHA'S   (n/r)

48 Shattuck Sq.   Berkeley   549-1814

Sujatha's combines erratic service with mundane atmosphere and mediocre food. Best for live entertainment (sarod and tabla) on Thursday night.

Hours: Daily 11-10.
Cards: All major.

## ROYAL INDIA   (n/r)

147 E. Third Ave.   San Mateo   348-3060

Pass.

Hours: M-Sa 12-3; 5:30-10; Su 5:30-10.
Cards: All major.

# SOUTHEAST ASIA

# 8. SOUTHEAST ASIA

### Burma • Cambodia • Laos

To many, Southeast Asia is among the most mysterious regions in the world. In the past decade or so, however, the Bay Area has gotten to know representatives of a couple of Southeast Asian countries--Vietnam and Thailand--quite well. In this part of the country at least, formerly unheard of items like *pad thai, sticky rice* and *lemongrass* are fast becoming household words. Since Thai and Vietnamese restaurants are so common here, they are not included in this book.

Until quite recently, no Southeast Asian countries except Vietnam and Thailand had made significant inroads on the American culinary scene-- not even in Northern California, where Asian cultures have traditionally taken root first. In the past few years, however, exponents of the cuisines of virtually the entire remainder of the Siamese peninsula, from Laos to Singapore, have sprung up around the Bay. Now virtually every Southeast Asian nation is represented by at least one restaurant here, and the national cuisines of two of these--Burma and Cambodia--probably have more exponents here than in the rest of the United States combined.

## BURMA

Like the country from which it hails, Burmese cuisine was all but unknown in the United States until a few years ago. In that short span, half a dozen Burmese restaurants have opened Bay Area doors. Most have been well received, and with good reason. Strategically situated between three culinary giants--China, Thailand and India--Burma has drawn from each while somehow managing to carve out its unique culinary identity.

### Appetizers, Soups and Salads

Nowhere is the "Western" influence on Burmese cuisine more obvious than with two appetizers typically associated with India and the Near East, respectively. *Samu-sa*--a deep-fried triangular turnover usually filled with curried potatoes or other vegetables--is a variant of Indian *samosa*. *Falafil*--fried split peas with spices--is a permutation of the

Middle Eastern *falafel*. Burma also imports *egg rolls* and *pot stickers* from China, and *pisang goreng* (fried bananas) from Malaysia. Perhaps the closest thing to an indigenous Burmese appetizer is *fried Burmese squash*.

Soups, however, are one of the strong suits on the Burmese menu. While there is no standard recipe for any particular Burmese soup, and you will encounter significant variations from restaurant to restaurant, there are some general types you will find at many Burmese places. In this group are *lemon grass, ong no kao*--coconut chicken soup, and *Burmese black pepper soup*--usually made with vegetables like squash, woodear mushrooms and bean curd as well as fish and vermicelli. The definitive Burmese soup, however (and the one to try if you are trying only one) is *curry fish noodle soup*--fish (often catfish) with ginger, garlic, noodles and cilantro. This is considered Burma's "national dish".

Burmese salads, often large and colorful as well as calculated to play mind games with your taste buds, are known for the divers ingredients which are put together on a single plate. Possibly the best example is *lap pat doke*. The primary ingredients in this "salad" are imported Burmese tea leaves, toasted lentil seeds, ground shrimp, fried garlic, sesame seeds and green peppers. *Ginger salad* offers the same type of diversity, but uses other ingredients like cabbage, peanuts, coconut and of course ginger. Other salads include *pig ear salad made with*--well, you guessed it.

### Entrées and Desserts

Since there are virtually no restaurants in Burma, to say that Burmese restaurant menus here tend to be "eclectic" would be something of an understatement. Nevertheless, while Burmese menus tend to be extremely diverse, you will notice at least a few dishes common to most of them. Three of these are curries: beef--sometimes served in a stew with lemon grass, tamarind and hot chili; chicken--often made with potatoes in coconut milk; and fish, possibly pompano, or *fish balls*. Other Burmese dishes you may be offered are a variety of noodle ones such as *onh no kaw*-- Burmese style coconut chicken. Many Burmese restaurants offer a full slate of Chinese fare as well.

At many a Southeast Asian restaurant, if you haven't achieved ecstasy by the time you've finished your main course, you aren't going to reach it there; but this is not necessarily true at Burmese restaurants, which often offer a wide selection of appealing closers. Perhaps the most interesting of these is *paluda*--a wonderful amalgam of coconut juice, paluda syrup, vanilla ice cream, tapioca and Burmese jello--baked with milk and eggs. Paluda is sometimes served in a "sundae" which may include such ingredients as red beans, grass jelly and roasted peanut ice cream. If you're favorite Burmese haunt is temporarily out of paluda, you wouldn't do badly to try either *jao jaw*--coconut jello, or *sui gi moke*--cream of wheat with poppy seeds and coconut milk.

## CAMBODIA

Although the recent proliferation of Southeast Asian restaurants has been a generalized phenomenon, no country has been more active on the Bay Area restaurant scene of late than Cambodia. Fueled in part by an influx of refugees from the Khmer Rouge "killing fields", the number of Cambodian restaurants has multiplied, in but a few short years, from just a couple to more than a dozen. This fact, coupled with the Cambodian reputation for alluring decor, superior service and quality cuisine has made Cambodia one of the rising stars on the local ethnic restaurant scene.

What to order? The Cambodian menu, like its Chinese counterpart, is typically huge. You might think you have so many choices that it will take forever to make up your mind. If you study your menu carefully, though, you will notice that within the many categories of Cambodian food--which are usually defined by their main constituent ingredient (e.g. *kari*--curry, or *moarn*--chicken)--often only a single word distinguishes one dish from another. The simple addition or subtraction of a spice may make two Cambodian dishes appear totally different. Thus, while in America *fried chicken* is called *fried chicken* whether it is seasoned with onion powder, chili powder or gunpowder; at Cambodian restaurants, a simple change in spice converts *chha morn somdech*--stir-fried chicken with pepper to *chha morn kyei*--stir-fried chicken with ginger.

Similarly, if you were to review a host of Cambodian menus simultaneously, you might think that none offer the same two dishes. While there is certainly more to distinguish the menus of Cambodian restaurants than say, Persian ones, they too tend to have much in common. Again, slight discrepancies may be accounted for by the substitution of one or two ingredients. Further, as the names of Cambodian dishes merely reflect their composite ingredients, it doesn't much matter to Cambodians in which order they are written. Thus, *chha sachko kreung* and *sach ko chhar kroeung* are precisely the same dish--stir-fried sliced beef with green peppers. Finally, the transliteration of Cambodian words into English is far from a exact science. So, whether you order *somlor maju pang pas* or *samlaw machou peng pos*, rest assured that you are ordering precisely the same thing--hot and sour soup with pineapple, vegetables and tamarind juice.

## ANGKOR PALACE {Cambodia} (9/9=18)

1769 Lombard St.   San Francisco   931-2830

Owner/chef Sony Sok, a real-life Dith Pran who, less than a decade ago was performing forced labor in the "killing fields", now oversees what is perhaps the Bay Area's premier Cambodian eating house. Angkor Palace, with its soft lights, sumptuous pillows and authentic Cambodian objets d'art makes a dazzling first, second and third impression. But what you'll really want to spend some time admiring are the restaurant's royal throne and what is, quite probably, this country's only display of wedding silver from the Royal Palace in Phnom Penh. Easily one of the most aesthetically appealing of all Bay Area ethnic restaurants, Angkor Palace also boasts some surprisingly innovative and wonderful Cambodian dishes. As far as appetizers go, deep-fried Cambodian style quail ($8.00) and Cambodian crepes in banchaw sauce ($5.00) are not all that out of the ordinary. However, the Palace also serves a couple of delightful appetizers we are not used to seeing, at least on Cambodian menus, such as *white fish* with bean sprouts and carrot threads ($6.00) and *escargot* ($12.00). Angkor Palace is also noteworthy for its panoply of fine Southeast Asian soups, the best of which may be *Cambodian fish chowder*--with mixed fish, shredded ginger and rice ($9.00), and *chicken-fruit soup*--green papaya bananas and pumpkin in broth ($8.00); as well as a few interesting salads. Try the *beef salad* with mint leaves and lemon grass ($5.00) or, if you are more daring, Angkor's *crispy ox tripe salad* with hot chili and "nightingale" sauce ($5.00). Of Angkor Palace's exhaustive list of entrees, the two which come most highly recommended are baked *stuffed chicken legs* ($9.00) and *its sizzling mixed seafood curry platter* ($12.00). Our personal favorites, however, are Battambang-style *chicken curry*--nicely served in a half coconut shell ($9.00), and *amok fish mousse*--a traditional Cambodian dish made with coconut milk and steamed in a banana leaf ($9.00). A variety of interesting and innovative vegetable dishes--including *winter melon and scrambled eggs,* and *steamed baby eggplants* (both $5.00)--are also served. Angkor's version of the customary Cambodian iced teas and coffees (made with cream and condensed milk--very rich, very fattening) are very good; but the restaurant falls down a bit with dessert, which basically boils down to ice cream and sherbet. In this one respect, several other Cambodian restaurants, with their *anoktis* (jackfruit) custards and pineapple pies are better.

Hours: Daily 5-11.
Cards: All major.

## ANGKOR BOREI {Cambodia} (7/10=17)

3471 Mission St.  San Francisco  550-8417

There are now a slew of Cambodian restaurants in the Bay Area and, with few exceptions, all are good--much better than the average ethnic restaurant. However, in some cases the atmosphere of Cambodian restaurants is a bit on the sterile side and their menus, though generally long, are often undistinguished. There are a number of exceptions to this rule--the city's popular Angkor Wat and Angkor Palace come to mind. However, if what you want is great Cambodian food at a reasonable price in a "regular" atmosphere, you will have to travel to a little known place called Angkor Borei. Compared to places like Angkors Palace and Wat, Borei is small and simple; but it does have a certain amount of charm--starting with a dazzling fire-eating dragon pagoda. Borei also displays gold-leaf ornamental paintings and traditional Cambodian placemats preserved under glass. Its ambience is also nice in other ways. For example, rice is beautifully served in a large silver urn, relaxing Cambodian music is played, and you won't find more hospitable service in too many places in or anywhere near the city. But it is in quality of cuisine that Borei can't be beat; especially for traditional Cambodian items such as *nohm ban jok*--homemade noodles with ground fish in a mild curry ($3.95). When we ordered this dish at proprietor Sonn Pok's suggestion, we weren't too optimistic. However, we wound up ordering seconds--it's that good. If you like curries, head straight for Borei's *kary morn*--curried chicken ($5.95). Flavored with such distinctly Southeast Asian spices as lemon grass, it is lighter and more texturous than the typical Indian curry and--since cooked carrots and zucchini are tossed in for flavor and texture--healthier too. In fact, even those who normally hate cooked garden vegetables may find them quite palatable when cooked in Borei's red coconut curry sauce. For a strictly vegetarian dish, we favor *char tofu*--sauteed soybean and other vegetables with yellow bean sauce served over rice. Even with shrimp added in this only costs $4.90--and it's good. Borei's piece d' resistance, however, is something you won't find on too many other Cambodian menus (although it occasionally turns up on a Filipino one)--*taro root pie*. Some South Indian restaurants use taro to make *patra*--a wonderful but somewhat heavy appetizer. As a dessert *taro* is even better--sweet and texturous as sweet potato pie, but with a unique and compelling flavor. At $1.75, taro pie is an excellent value, too.

Hours: Daily 11-10.
Cards: V/MC/AE.

## MANDALAY RESTAURANT {Burma} (8/8=16)

4344 California St.   San Francisco   386-3895

Hanging coconuts, sequined art work, balloons, chinese lanterns, and hanging plants all pleasantly combine in this, San Francisco's premiere Burmese restaurant. Its atmosphere is attractive enough, even if the place at times seems a bit too Chinese; and service is wonderful. Mandalay's primary attraction is its diverse, interesting and, generally speaking, quite flavorful food. For starters, you might try *samu sa*--ground curried meat and onions in a fried wrapping ($2.00), then proceed to one of the restaurant's many unusual salads, perhaps *lap pat dok*--which consists of imported Burmese tea leaves toasted with lentil seeds, ground shrimps, and sesame seeds ($5.95). These ingredients are mixed and mashed by your waiter right at your table--a must experience. Although Mandalay provides a huge array of homemade soups to choose from, we most like *chin hin yee*--a hot and sour broth with lemon grass and fish ($4.50). Among Mandalay's other innovative soups are *ong nu hin yee*--coconut chicken soup ($4.75), and *black pepper soup*--featuring vegetables, squash vermicelli and rock cod filet ($4.50). The fowl of choice are *chicken mandalay*--slices of fried chicken sauteed with garlic in a tangy hot sauce ($6.75), and R*angoon smoked duck* served with Burmese tea leaves ($17.00 whole). Although Mandalay also offers a number of beef items, we prefer their seafood offerings such as *nga pe dok*--a Burmese-style fish cake with salad, cilantro, and crunchy garlic chips ($5.95). Also interesting is M*andalay squid* ($6.50)--which features chewy calamari served on a bed of spinach topped with fried onion and a hot and sour sauce. Finally, our vegetable dish of the month goes to *chin mong jaw*--a leafy, sour Burmese vegetable akin to mint, which is sauteed with prawns and bamboo shoots ($5.50). While at dessert time some Southeast Asian restaurants come up a little lame, not so Mandalay. *Sug gi mok* (6 pieces for $2.50) is a can't miss item made from cream of wheat, coconut milk and poppy seeds. Another find is *paluda* ice cream---made from tapioca, coconut juice, paluda syrup, chopped roasted peanuts and a dollop of vanilla ($2.95). Drinks are also a novelty at Mandalay. Although iced red bean drink ($1.50) is an acquired taste, and is occasionally found at other Southeast Asian restaurants, you won't see a tapioca and coconut drink ($1.50) on too many other menus, and you won't have to learn to like it either--its divine.

Hours: Daily 11-9:45.
Cards: V/MC.

## LAN XANG {Laos} (8/8=16)

5336 Geary Blvd.   San Francisco   752-4310

Possibly the only authentic Laotian restaurant in the nation, Lan Xang is neither ornate nor elaborate, but is nevertheless an interesting and peaceful, almost monastic little place. With bamboo mats, trays--bamboo everything--you feel at Lan Xang like you've stepped right out of San Francisco and into the Mekong delta. Soothing strains of Southeast Asian music lull you into the proper frame of mind to enjoy what, in all probability, will be your inaugural experience with Lao cuisine. But reserve your kudos for Lan Xang's incredible edibles, starting with an appetizer of barbecued beefballs with sugar cane sauce. Then comes a choice of a half dozen unique salads including *tom maak hoong*--papaya, carrot, dried shrimp and chili (delicious--$3.95). Now, how about barbequed catfish or, better, *ping goong*--charbroiled prawns ($9.95)? Lan Xang also has a flair for deep-fried dishes like butterfish, angle prawns and *ping kha gob*--frog legs in a spicy lime sauce ($6.95). Try it.

Hours: Daily 11-3, 5-10.
Cards: V, MC.

## NAN YANG {Burma} (7/9=16)

301 Eighth St.   Oakland   465-6924

Simple touches like Burmese pagoda pictures, wicker lamps and peaceful music distinguish Nan Yang from the run of the mill restaurants of Oakland's Chinatown. The brainchild of Burmese architect Philip Chu, who may be single-handedly responsible for introducing Burmese cuisine to Northern California, Nan Yang was the Bay Area's first Burmese restaurant (circa. 1982). While not as ornate as Mandalay, Nan Yang arguably serves the Bay Area's best Burmese food, including such lovelies as fried tropical squash, green mango and papaya salad, curry fish soup, curried okra, and tapioca pudding with coconut milk. Lunch is a good deal (try the Nan Yang combination--with Malay curried chicken, Indian samosa and jumbo prawns--$4.25), but more Burmese specialties are offered at night. For an interesting change of pace, try *congee*--rice porridge, with your choice of fillers. Nan Yang is one of Oakland's better ethnic restaurants and far and away the best one in Chinatown.

Hours: Tu-Th; F-Sa 11-9:30; Su-11-9;.
Cards: V/MC.

## BAYON {Cambodia} (7/7=14)

2018 Lombard St.  San Francisco  922-1400

    This is one of those places that make you wonder if subjectively rating ethnic restaurants is truly possible. A Southeast Asian restaurant serving "California/Cambodian cuisine" in the "traditional aristocratic French style?" Unlike most restaurants which try to appeal to too many tastes, Bayon, to some extent, succeeds. Understated Cambodian music and superb service complement an atmosphere just Asian enough to make the place seem genuine--sort of the way you would have expected to feel in a superior French restaurant in Phnom Penh before the war. Many of Bayon's dishes are served *katis*--that is, in a sauce made from coconut milk, lemongrass and other spices. *Chicken katis* is a fairly common Cambodian dish, but Bayon offers some other items which are not often prepared in this style like poached salmon ($12.00), escargots ($6.00 as an appetizer) and frog's legs ($14.00). The truly gutsy won't pass up the chance to try *khuor ko*--calf's brains in lime ($12.00). We did, however.

Hours: Tu-Sa 5:30-10:30; Su 4:30-9:30.
Cards: All major.

## THE CAMBODIANAS {Cambodia} (5/8=13)

2156 University Ave.  Berkeley  (843-4630)

    Maybe it's the delightful costumes worn by proprietor Linsu Ke's family, who wait on you, or the fresh flowers on every table; or maybe it's Ke's excellent cooking, but--despite the complete absence of anything on its walls--there is something light, airy and authentic about this otherwise simple, modern and not overly compelling Cambodian haunt. (Actually the fact that The Cambodianas' walls are bare comes as something of a relief given that the building's former occupant--an otherwise excellent Cambodian place called Chumno Paillin--had decorated with somewhat macabre pictures of headless and/or limbless statues). This is Ke's second Bay Area venture. The first, Monorum, was a small but popular restaurant near Daly City. This one is just as good, with some superb fresh vegetable dishes and excellent sauces. Our favorite is Cambodian-style rabbit in coconut sauce ($9.50). A combination lunch special permits two to try a variety of specialties for only $12.00.

Hours: Daily 11:30-10.
Cards: All major.

## PHNOM PENH HOUSE  {Cambodia}  (6/7=13)

251 Eighth St.   Oakland   893-3826

Virtually everything in Phnom Penh House bespeaks the profound attachment its original owner, and seemingly all Cambodians, feel towards Cambodia, Phnom Penh, and especially Angkor Wat--Cambodia's colossal ruined wonder--which you can catch glimpses of in posters, postcards, and even a colorful hand-carved plastic ornament which runs the restaurant's entire perimeter. This pride in all things Cambodian also translates into some pretty fair Cambodian food. We particularly like *trei chean bonlai kreun*--deep-fried red snapper with bean thread noodles in ginger sauce ($7.25) and *moarn ann kreun*--barbequed chicken with lemon grass ($4.65). Both of Phnom Penh's desserts: *susa*--a sort of coconut gelatin trifle vaguely reminiscent of Peruvian *alfajores*, and *chhet chean*--heavily fried bananas coated with coconut and served with vanilla ice cream (1.95)-- are excellent. The downside is that this restaurant--being good, cheap, well respected, and small--can get pretty crowded on weekends.

Hours: M-Th 11-9:30; F-Sa 11-10.
Cards: MC/V.

## BAKSEY CHAM KRONG  {Cambodia}  (5/7=12)

1770 Haight St.   San Francisco   387-9224

Baksey Cham Krong--a modern and chic place perched on a second story landing above Haight Street--is a good spot to sample some pretty fair examples of Cambodian cooking, starting with *segs sur bang korng*--deep-fried quail with lemon sauce ($7.50). Some unusual pork entrees are served including *trorp trung kroeung*--baked eggplant topped with shrimp and ground pork in garlic sauce ($6.25) and *prahok kroeung*--ground pork with anchovies, red curry and coconut milk ($5.95). Only the stoutest of heart (no pun intended) will want to try *bor bor chheam chhroukk*--pork intestines, heart, liver and blood--a Cambodian specialty; but, if you like your food spicy, you might enjoy one of Baksey's original Cambodia style curries, perhaps *saramann*--beef with mild red curry, onion and coconut milk. Lunch specials (predominantly soups) are extremely reasonable (about $4.00). Although not indicated on the menu, a delicious heavy cream Cambodian Iced Tea is also available.

Hours: Daily 5-10:30 (exc. F until 11).
Cards: V/MC/AE.

## ON LOK YUEN {Burma} (6/6=12)

3721 Geary Blvd. San Francisco 386-6208

Elephant paintings adorn this quaint Burmese place which feels somewhat similar to nearby "Burma" but, with lace curtains and a classic Burmese altar, is a bit more elegant. Try the *curried fish balls* ($6.25).

Hours: M-Tu 5-9:30; W-Th 11:30-9:30; F-Su 11:30-10:30.
Cards: V/MC.

## PHNOM PENH {Cambodia} (5/6=11)

631 Larkin St. San Francisco 775-5979

Pan fried catfish, stuffed eggplant, grilled red snapper, and *papaya salad* are some of the interesting specialties at this simple but pleasant place. Dinners are reasonable ($6.95--$9.95), and lunch is even more so.

Hours: M-Th 11-9:30; F-Sa 11-10.
Cards: V/MC/AE.

## BURMA RESTAURANT {Burma} (5/5=10)

309 Clement St. San Francisco 751-4091

Not as atmospheric as other Bay Area Burmese restaurants, but not bad. Try Burma's *dunpao rice with curried beef and potatoes* ($6.25) and *sui gi moke*--cream of wheat, coconut milk and poppy seeds ($2.50).

Hours: M-Sa 11-9:30.
Cards: AE.

## SAYONN'S {Cambodia} (n/r)

824 University Ave. Berkeley 843-1189

One of the least exciting of the Bay Area's good crop of Southeast Asian restaurants. Nothing special either by way of ambience or cuisine.

Hours: Tu-F 11:30-2:30, 5-10; F-Sa 5-11.
Cards: All major.

# THE PACIFIC RIM

# PACIFIC RIM

Australia • Indonesia • Korea • The Philippines

To many Americans, the Far East connotes the ultimate in world travel; and it is here, on the Pacific Rim, that we make our final stop before returning to the Western Hemisphere and home. Many Pacific Rim nations--such as New Zealand, New Guinea and Micronesia--have no Bay Area representatives. Others like China and Japan have far too many for us to be able to do an adequate job of reviewing them here. Thus, in this chapter, we will focus on the cuisines of three major Asian nations--Indonesia, the Philippines and Korea; and one comparatively minor Oceanic one--Australia.

## INDONESIA

From the ultra-modern Southeast Asian city of Singapore, right at the tip of the Malay Peninsula, it is but a skip and jump across the Strait of Malacca to Sumatra--the largest of Indonesia's famed "Spice Islands", and the beginning of our adventure in the nations of the Pacific Rim. Although the world's fifth most populous country, Indonesia has made little impact upon the American culinary scene. Numerous visits to several of this country's few Indonesian establishments have failed to explain this phenomenon to us. When done up right--with thatched bamboo ceilings, torches and hypnotic gamelan music--the ambience of Indonesian restaurants can be among the most spectacular of any in the world. The cuisine of Indonesia too, while unfamiliar to most Americans, is distinctive and profoundly imaginative.

Indonesia's national motto is "unity in diversity" and indeed, from both a religious and cultural perspective, there is a great deal of diversity to unite. The nation's cuisine reflects similar variety. Sumatrans tend to like their foods spicy. Chili and tumeric flavor their Indian-like curries known as *gulais*. To the east the Javanese, like many Chinese, favor sweet and sour dishes; but, as they are by and large Muslims, they don't eat pork. At the eastern tip of Java is the predominantly Hindu isle of Bali, where pork is eaten; while people from Borneo, north of Java, enjoy foods similar to those consumed in Malaysia.

## Soups, Salads, Appetizers and Spice

It was Marco Polo who gave Indonesia its "Spice Islands" appellation. With superabundant supplies of such popular flavor-enhancers as cloves, nutmeg, pepper, ginger and cinnamon, the name is apt. Other foodstuffs which add a distinctive lilt to Indonesian fare are tamarind, coconut, sereh--lemon grass and kecap--soy sauce. Also popular in Indonesia, but a rarity here, are blachan. These dried, salted shrimps are allowed to rot before being eaten.

Although you'll occasionally be served laksa--a coconut-based soup with prawns, tamarind, bean curd, vegetables, chicken and noodles--at Indonesian restaurants soups are not the main attraction. Indonesia does boast a popular and interesting salad, however. Known as *gado-gado*, this is a potpourri made from such ingredients as cucumber, tomato, sprouts, egg--lots of egg--and, most importantly, peanut sauce. Two other salads you will sometimes come across are *rujak*--a spicy fruit and vegetable salad with peanut sauce, and *acar campur*--pickled vegetable salad.

Peanut sauce is widely used throughout Southeast Asia, but it is exalted in Indonesia, where it has been given a special name--*satay*. *Satay* is also the name of a popular Indonesian dish of broiled meat basted in peanut sauce which, traditionally, is served on bamboo skewers. Although usually a main course in Indonesia, here *satay* is often served as an appetizer. Other common Indonesian appetizers are *sumpia*--which are similar to Chinese egg rolls but lighter, crispier and often served in satay; *serundeng*--fried coconut shreds with peanuts; and *krupuk*--shrimp toast. Occasionally you may be offered *pergedel*--spiced potato cakes; *martabak*--stuffed pancake rolls or *udang assam manis*--sweet and sour prawns.

## Entrees, Beverages and Desserts

Since most Indonesians, unlike Indians, are Muslims, they do eat beef; but, except for satay, you will not see much of it. The same is true for shrimp and fish, which you would expect to see a lot more of from an island nation. Indonesia's most popular meats are *ayam*--chicken, and *kambing*--lamb. Popular Indonesian *chicken* dishes include *ayam kuri*--curried chicken; *ayam opor*--chicken in coconut sauce; *ayam rujak*--chicken in a spicy paprika sauce; and *ayam goreng*--fried chicken, Java-style. Indonesia's most popular lamb dish is *kare kambing*--curried lamb.

Like Indians, Indonesians make wonderful use of vegetables. The dishes to look for are *sajur lodeh*--vegetables in coconut sauce; *sajur rujak*--vegetables in paprika sauce; and *sajur kari*--vegetable curry. Even better are Indonesia's *nasi (*rice) and *bami (*noodle) combinations called *nasi* and *bami rames*. *Nasi rames* is a plate of rice topped with various vegetables, meats and sauce. Bami rames is similar, but with noodles.

In addition to prodigious amounts of coffee and tea, Indonesians drink many tropical juices, such as *cocos*--coconut, *asam*--tamarind, and *sirsak*--guanabana. The most common Indonesian desserts are *paluda*-- an iced noodle dessert similar to Persian and Indian *falooda*, *agar-agar*--a flavored jello-like little morsel, and *pisang goreng*--fried bananas.

Many Indonesian restaurants offer guests the opportunity to simultaneously sample a wide variety and enormous quantity of diverse specialties, usually in only slightly smaller portions than if each individual item was ordered a la carte. This feast, called a *rijstaffel (rice table)*, affords an enjoyable way to experience a whole host of foods you probably have never tried anything quite like before. Note, however, that while the *rijstaffel* is an Indonesian innovation, Indonesians tend to associate it with colonial Dutch domination. Thus, although frequently served both here and in Europe, the *rijstaffel* is not too popular in its birthplace right now.

## AUSTRALIA

Many people do not realize that only a brief boat ride from the southern Indonesian island of Timor separates Indonesia from a new country--Australia, and a different continent--Oceania. However, Australian cuisine bears little resemblance to any of the indigenous cuisines of Australia's own hemisphere. For that reason, and because there is, at present, only one Australian restaurant of note in the Bay Area, we will discuss Australia within the confines of that review.

## THE PHILIPPINES

Thirty degrees north and slightly west of Darwin, in Northern Australia, lies Manila, the capital and cultural heart of another major Pacific Rim nation, the Philippines. Although the Philippines boasts a wide variety of dishes unique to the Far East, perhaps no other country's cuisine (except perhaps our own) is more indebted to outside influences--a reflection of the Philippines' historical domination by such powerful neighbors as China, Japan and Korea; as well as its more recent colonization by (or "protection" from) first Spain, then the United States.

Of all the influences on Filipino culture, none is more deeply-rooted than the Spanish, which permeates every aspect of Filipino life, including its foods--many of which are still called by Spanish names. Certainly, if you were told that you were going to be taken to a restaurant where you would be served appetizers like *tocino* (pork) and *gambas* (prawns)--followed by entrees like *lengua* (beef tongue), *menudo* (pork in tomato sauce), and *arroz caldo* (rice porridge)--you would not be apt to think you would be dining at a representative of a Far Eastern nation. But--whether indigenous to the Philippines or the product of a foreign power's influence--Filipino dishes are undeniably diverse and interesting, and well worth getting to know.

### Pampagana (Appetizers)

Probably the most common Filipino appetizer is *lumpia*--spring rolls, which are frequently stuffed with beef, onions and raisins. *Siopao*--pork or chicken buns, are sometimes served as *pampagana* and sometimes as *matamis*--desserts. Also, you may occasionally come across such beguiling appetizers as *chitcharon bulaklak*--crispy pork innards, *tokwa't baboy*--tofu and pork, or *camaron rebosado*--breaded shrimps.

### Entrees and Matamis (Desserts)

Perhaps the definitive Filipino main courses are *adobo*--slices of meat (usually pork or chicken) in a sour sauce; *pancit*--thin noodles often mixed with items such as *sontanghon* (mung bean), *bihon* (rice sticks) or *gulay* (vegetables); *bangus*--milkfish, served either *daing*--deep fried, or *sinigang*--in a sour broth; and *pinkabet*--mixed vegetables in sauce with shrimp or anchovies. However, there are a host of other appealing Filipino entrees including *escabeche*--pickled halibut with ginger; *asado*--slices of beef with soy; *estofado*--beef with olives, potatoes, peppers and pickles in a sweet and sour sauce; *tapas*--seasoned slices of beef or pork, sometimes served with *atsara* (pickled papaya); *kalderetang*--goat meat stew; and *sarciado*--sauteed chunks of meat and vegetables in spices. Also not to be missed are traditional Filipino dishes like *apritadang manok*--chicken stew; *kare-kare*--ox-tail in peanut sauce; and one which, outside of Filipino restaurants, you won't see every day: *dinuguan*--pork in chocolate sauce.

The definitive Filipino dessert is *halo halo*--a refreshing combination of shaved ice, mixed fruit and milk. Others worth a try are *leche flan*--a derivative of the famous Spanish milk custard, but richer; *turon*--plantain bananas; and *gulaman atsaya*--agar agar with tapioca--a dish Filipinos share their love for with Indonesians.

## KOREA

Due north of the Philippines lies another intriguing Pacific Rim nation--Korea--and its highly innovative national cuisine. Since, in Korea, there are no "courses"--all foods being served at the same time--Koreans do not categorize their dishes as "appetizers","soups", "salads" and the like. Instead, Korean dishes tend to be grouped according to how they are prepared--e.g. "broiled", "griddled", "pan-fried" or in a "casserole".

While, as an accommodation to their American guests, many Bay Area Korean restaurants do *serve* appetizers, since Koreans themselves do not eat them there is little rhyme or reason as to which items will be offered as appetizers at any given restaurant. Some may offer *yukhweh*--seasoned raw beef, *honguh-hweh*--raw skate or pan-fried green onions. As a further accommodation to Western tastes, some may serve *goon mandu*--pot stickers.

Another distinctive aspect of the Korean meal is that each entree is accompanied by an assortment of condiments, sometimes 10 or more, which vary, but usually include indigenous Korean items such as *kim chee* (pickled cabbage), dried anchovies and bean sprouts. Koreans always eat these dishes together with their main courses. Nonetheless, since many Americans incorrectly presume that these condiments are "appetizers", Korean proprietors accustomed to receiving American guests may serve them before the meal, appetizer-style.

The number of entrees on most Korean menus is vast, and you could go into most Korean restaurants 30 or 40 times without ever feeling compelled to order the same dish twice. Indeed, Korean restaurants tend to offer the same basic foods in more ways than some restaurants offer different types of foods. That said, there are certain dishes common to most Korean restaurants, and some that are particularly well suited to the occidental palate.

Of these, three meat dishes--*kal-bi*, *bul-go-ki* and *bi-bim-bab*--stand out. Bul-go-ki, the Korean national dish, consists of tender slices of beef which are marinated in a special sauce, then barbecued--often times by you, yourself, at your very own table. *Kal-bi* is similar, except that instead of strips of beef you get short ribs, which can be quite chewy and are therefore often better when served in soup (*kal-bi-tang*). *Bi-bim-bab*, more spicy than either *bul-go-ki* or *kal-bi*, consists of beef and vegetables served with a fried egg on top.

One of our favorite Korean items is not a specific thing, but a type of thing. Referred to alternately as a *casserole or* a *hot pot*, this is--as its name suggests--a crock of extremely hot soup, most times served with its innards still boiling. As to what is in the soup, you will often have a number of choices. Where available, our favorite *hot pot* contains bean curd and clams, but we have had others such as anchovy and tripe, and they have all been interesting.

Other common Korean main courses include *kal gook soo*--hand cut noodle soup; *kimchee-jige*--pickled cabbage casserole; *bokumbab*--Korean fried rice; *mandoo-gook*--dumpling soup; *dak-gu-i*--chopped roast chicken; *jap chae bap*--low calorie noodles with beef; *bi bim nang*--cold noodles in spicy sauce; *joki-gu-i*--salted kingfish; and *o-jin-gu-i*--squid in hot sauce. This list is by no means meant to be exhaustive and, in fact, you may visit some restaurants which offer few of these.

Then there are a series of traditional Korean dishes which, you are sometimes warned, are "for the more adventurous palate only". Almost all Korean restaurants offer a variety of such entrees (although you may not always be warned). These tend to be spicy hot and/or very unfamiliar to Westerners. For example, you will sometimes come across *gomtang*--a spicy Korean beef and tripe soup; *kori gomtang*--the same, with oxtail; *ke jang*--spicy raw crab; or *pork blood soup*.

After the Korean meal some sort of fruit, usually apples, is served. There is no such thing as a Korean "pastry tray", and few Korean restaurants serve anything which remotely resembles a typical American sweet. If you enquire, however, you may find that *shik hae* (rice punch) is available. This is an interesting and aromatic beverage generally drunk from a bowl.

## RICE TABLE (THE) {Indonesia} (10/9=19)

1617 Fourth St. San Rafael 456-1808

It doesn't take long to feel like you're on a travel once you set foot in the door of the "Rice Table". Two carved heads stand guard over a wall of bamboo. Inside, four ceiling fans hanging from rafters that would have done a Bogart movie justice swirl above you, and bamboo booths, carvings, wicker lamps, embossed glass tables, and gold-laminated paintings await. Tropically-adorned waiters move about the Rice Table with an air of meditative dignity. From a culinary standpoint, the Rice Table serves extremely good, although pretty standard, Indonesian fare. If you are a Southeast Asia veteran and very game, try the "hot" *Ayam Pangang*--barbecued chicken smothered in soy sauce. The very hungry but more timid of palate will want to try the Rice Table Dinner ($12.95 per person), which includes some wafer thin *sumpia*, *satay*, *udang*--shrimp fried in tamarind, *keri ayam*--mild chicken curry, *semur*--bits of beef cooked in cloves and soy sauce, and *bihen goreng*--fried rice noodles. Of course, these are just the entrees. As with all *rijstaffels*, a parade of appetizers precede them, along with soup, *krupuk*--shrimp toast, two types of salad, rice and an excellent fried banana for dessert. To wash all of this good eating down, *asam*--tamarind juice ($1.00) is a must. Also, try to save some room for the Rice Table's fine *coffee tubruk* (also $1.00). This is Indonesian-style coffee made fresh from ground java beans--among the world's richest. Like all *rijstaffels* both here and abroad, there is far too much food for two people too eat. But, don't worry. While some restaurants treat people who ask for doggie bags like lepers, the Rice Table staff treats a doggie bag request by preparing a parcel that would shame U.P.S. It makes you feel like, if this is the way they treat *leftovers*, what pains must they take the first time around? If you want to find out, all you have to do is make a pretense of washing up. To get to the washroom--uniquely positioned in the family garage--you have to pass through the Rice Table kitchen. Take a moment, if you will, and watch. Each Rice Table meal is prepared with the same meticulous attention to detail. You'll feel like you are having dinner at the home of a group of family friends who both know how to cook and really care about pleasing you. Don't miss this one.

Hours: Th-Sa 5:30-10; Su 5-9.
Cards: All Major.

## THE AUSTRALIAN {Australia} (9/8=17)

898 Lincoln Ave.  San Jose  (408) 293-1112

There are so few restaurants run by expatriate Aussies that proprietor Claude Anthony could call his Willow Glen establishment *the* Australian Restaurant without much fear of contradiction. Although off the beaten track, the Australian is one of those rare places that warrants a special trip. We've been to the Australian several times over the years but, when we first visited, our initial reaction was one of disappointment. Posters--some rather tacky--covered its walls and ceiling, and electronic games were lined up in the rear. All dressed up, we felt out of place--like a couple of yahoos who'd accidentally stepped into a kicker bar. But our discomfort didn't last long. "G'day!" Anthony boomed from across the room. "What'll it be?" It took us awhile to warm up to the raucous, fun-loving crowd, but we did. It didn't hurt that the Australian's food is good, fresh, and cheap, as well as being an authentic recreation of down under pub grub. Fifteen bucks bought a huge plate of cottage pie (like England's shepherd's pie), an Aussie meat pie, two glasses of birch beer and a wonderful box of Arnott's cookies. The Aussie meat pie is deserving of its acclaim as Australia's national dish. Though its innards look and taste like those of a regular pot pie, its top crust is more like that of a puff pastry or souffle, and it is delicious. Other Aussie dishes worth a try are *snag'll do*--braised bangers (sausages) in tomato sauce, and *bush-wacker*--beef and vegetables over rice. More traditional English items, like cottage pie and pasties, are also available and also good. The cookies were served to us on a dare. Anthony had just finished glowingly described the rich whipped *pavlovas* (tortes) he *used* to make. Then he said he no longer takes the trouble to make them because, once his customers finish their hearty entrees, they are too full for dessert. By this time, however, we were primed for an Australian sweet treat. So Anthony broke out a box of imported Arnott's biscuits. "Here mates", he said, "try a couple of these. If you like em, buy em. If not, I'll eat 'em meself, I will!". When an ethnic restaurant has you rethinking your vacation plans you know you've stumbled across a great one. Throughout our meal all we talked about was travelling to Australia. When we finally reluctantly dragged ourselves out of the Australian, feeling full and edified and alive, we peered back at the tongue-in-cheek sign that used to hang in front of Anthony's simple but popular store: "eat here before we both starve" it said. Good natured Aussie humor. Well worth the trip.

Hours: Tu-F 10-8; Sa 2-8.
Cards: No.

## THE PHILIPPINE {The Philippines} (8/8=16)

3619 Balboa Ave. San Francisco 752-8657

Many Filipino restaurants reflect their nations' melting pot heritage, but "the Philippines"--with overhanging trellises, Christmas lights, overhead lamps that don't match, and posters explaining the evolution of the Filipino flag--is really a sight. Foodwise, the Philippines offers an enormous selection of authentic Filipino dishes prepared with painstaking (and sometimes lugubriously slow) effort. We can't complain about the delay, however, because you are forewarned before you order that "we cannot sacrifice the quality by being rushed". Start off with *lumpiang shanghai*--spring rolls with beef and raisins. Of the numerous entree possibilities, you might try *kari-kari*--oxtails in a bubbling sauce with *bagoong*--shrimp paste ($7.99), or *sinigang na bangus*--milkfish in tamarind broth ($8.99). Lack of authentic music hurts but this is definitely a travel--the type of place you don't often find in your neighborhood, won't find two of, and don't come across every day.

Hours: W-Sa 1-10; Su 3-8.
Cards: None. No checks. Accepts cash.

## PADANG {Indonesia} (8/7=15)

700 Post St. San Francisco 775-6708

From the outside, Padang looks great--quaint and authentic. Your expectations are somewhat diminished, however, when you sit down and listen to the music. Instead of Indonesia's wonderful, peaceful, and almost mystical *gamelan* music, you are treated to something that sounds vaguely like Barbara Streisand singing in Chinese. Padang is attractively decorated, however, and its meals are very good. If you've never experienced Indonesian food, you simply must try the *rijstaffel here*. Padang's version ($10.25) features 10 courses, each of which is better than the next. You start with a noodle broth. No, you don't have a cold. It *is* tasteless. Padang's *gado gado* is better, but not by much. Some of its main courses are excellent, however; including *ayam kari*--curried chicken, and *nasi rames*--fried rice. Also, if you want to convince someone that Southeast Asians know how to make good desserts, Padang is a good place to go. Try the *agar-agar*.

Hours: M-Sa 5-10; Tu-F 11:30-2.
Cards: All major.

## PO SEOK CHUNG {Korea} (8/7=15)

1437 Harrison St.   Oakland   763-6255

A beautifully carved wooden interior, some appealing Korean objets d'art including a tansu, and several very attractive hand-painted Korean dried gourds called "paks" decorate this roomy, pleasant new place located in the heart of downtown Oakland. Po Seok Chung offers traditional Korean fare plus a few surprises, including *jok tang*--"beef feet" soup (7.50), and popular favorites such as *gal bee tang*--short ribs in soup. Another tasty morsel at Po Seok Chung is its *bean dae duk*--a traditional Korean pancake made from ground mung bean, meat and vegetables ($4.50). Po Seok Chung also features an exquisite beverage-dessert, *sujung gwa*--persimmon and ginger ($1.95), as well as a refreshing *shik hae*--rice punch. Service is good and uniformly friendly.

Hours: Daily 11-10.
Cards: V/MC/AE.

## SORABOL {Korea} (7/8=15)

372 Grand Ave.   Oakland   839-2288

One of the best of the Bay Area's burgeoning number of Korean restaurants, Sorabol--a popular but peaceful Korean sanctuary where everything from its music down to the pastel animal prints on its walls is soft--has just enough Koreabilia to make you feel like you're somewhere exotic. Though more formal than the run of the mill Korean barbecue houses which have been springing up around the Bay of late, Sorabol remains sedate and relaxed. Carved brown wood beams throughout give the impression of dining in a peaceful Korean tea house. Service is excellent and Sorabol's food is both above average and well served. A couple of its most interesting items are *neng myun*--buckwheat noodles in a cold beef broth ($7.95), and *junbok guyee*--broiled abalone in hot sauce ($12.95). There are also many nice small touches at Sorabol. For example, after your meal, tea is served in a glass held by a little wicker basket.

Hours: Daily 11-9:30.
Cards: All major.

## TITO REY OF THE ISLANDS {Philippines} (6/8=14)

3 St Francis Square   Daly City   756-2870

Until you pay a visit to Tito Rey on the weekend, you may not realize just how large a Filipino population the Bay area has. On any given Friday or Saturday night, however, you're apt to find a significant number of these crammed into Tito's cavernous restaurant/night club enjoying typical Filipino entertainment. While unquestionably the Bay Area's definitive Filipino restaurant--with sister restaurants in Los Angeles, Washington and Manila--Tito Rey isn't going to break any records for homeyness and charm. Tito offers an uncompromising menu with such novel Filipino favorites as *dinuguan*--roast pork in chocolate sauce. But, even though Tito Rey's authentic menu and huge Filipino throng may make you feel like you're on a travel to the Far East, you won't particularly feel like this is the place you'd want to be when you get there.

Hours: Daily 11-11.
Cards: All major.

## SAHRANG BAHNG {Korea} (6/8=14)

2505D Hearst Ave.   Berkeley   486-1900

You probably wouldn't expect to find a good, authentic Korean restaurant within a block of U. C. Berkeley but with Sahrang Bahng-- tucked away in a corner of a Northside mini-mall--what you see is what you get. What you see are bamboo mats and calligraphy prints--more Japanese than Korean--and a whole lot of Korean students savoring some of the East Bay's best Korean fare. What you get is excellent food and service. Appetizers include a series of "pancakes" which are more like fritters--try Sahrang's mushroom pancake ($2.50). Our favorite main course is *kal bi*--barbecued short ribs ($5.95), although Sahrang's *jap chae*-- vegetable beef vermicelli is also quite good. As befits a campus locale, portions are ample and prices are obscenely cheap (e.g sake--$1.25).

Hours: Daily 10-9.
Cards: None. Accepts personal checks.

## KENKOY'S DINER {The Philippines} (8/6=14)

54 Mint St.   San Francisco   957-0404

No mistaking the cultural identity of this place. If scores of Filipino patrons don't mark this as an authentic establishment, then a huge Filipino flag, a sign announcing a "jeepney" stop, and hordes of license plates from such places as Manila and Quezon City will. Tucked away on a little side street behind the U.S. mint, there is absolutely nothing about Kenkoy's calculated to attract the attention of San Francisco's non-Filipino business community. This fact seems to suit owner Frank "Kenkoy" (after a famous Filipino cartoon character) Torres and his loyal Filipino clientele just fine. Meals are served cafeteria-style and there is no menu so, if you don't speak the Filipino language, you're not likely to know what your choices are. Do what you'd do if you were in Laoag City. Point. At the least, you'll be able to identify *shrimp pancit* ($2.75), which is excellent. Kenkoy's also serves a mean *rice pie* ($.75) and there's plenty of *halo halo* ($2.00) in the frig. For the rest you'll just have to experiment.

Hours: Daily 7(a)-6(p).
Cards: None.

## KOREAN CABIN {Korea} (6/8=14)

2170 Mission St.   San Francisco   626-6236

One of the most original of the Bay Area's Korean restaurants, the Korean Cabin looks like exactly what it is--an attractively renovated Filipino cafeteria. The elaborate interior hand-carved woodwork so common at "better" Korean restaurants is conspicuously absent from the Cabin, and you won't find any antique tansus, Korean bowing dolls, or "paks". However, the restaurant is presided over by one of the Bay Area's most personable proprietors, Jong Kim (no relation to the North Korean premier), and it boasts some nice, simple decorations--among them lots of plants and a display of Jong's own paintings. Also unique is Jong's offering of *monk's food*--a slate of unusual vegetarian dishes including *dark wheat noodle with vegetables* and *stir fried potato starch*. More traditional items include an excellent bean curd hot pot ($5.50). Although good and extremely interesting, our fear is that the fledgling restaurant may have a tough time surviving in its non-Korean Mission District locale.

Hours: Daily 11-11.
Cards: V/MC.

## KING SE-JONG {Korea} (7/6=13)

22507 Main St.   Fremont   538-1234

This tastefully designed and decorated restaurant has just about everything you might expect--some fine hand-carved wood, a flowing fountain stocked with fish, an electrically operated Korean bowing doll, and more pretty "paks"--intricately carved hand-painted dried pumpkins--than just about any other Korean restaurant around. As with other Korean haunts, King's American-style music is a turnoff, and the restaurant's atmosphere is far from pert. Still, King Se-Jeong is more aesthetically pleasing than most Korean barbecue house, and service is a bit better too. The restaurant's large menu contains the usual complement of barbecued dishes, as well as an assortment of "traditional" dinners, at least some of which--such as *cooked blood soup* ($7.75) and *spicy tripe casserole for two* ($19.95)--you are not likely to have tasted before. The best value on the menu is the *Se Joeng Dinner*, featuring dumpling soup, griddled oysters, and an assortment of barbecued meats ($24.95 for two).

Hours: M-Sa 11:30-10; Su 1-10.
Cards: V/MC. No checks.

## CARINDERIA {The Philippines} (6/6=12)

214 Townsend St.   San Francisco   957-1129

Talk about an unprepossessing little place. Although you can judge some restaurants by their cover, Carinderia is full of surprises. The first is that the restaurant's tiny storefront (from the outside, it looks more like a butcher shop than a restaurant) opens to a backyard patio which, in good weather, is full of blooming fuchsia and lilacs. A kitten lazily suns itself while a blackbird harmonizes with gently tinkling wind chimes from the restaurant next door. This may not be The Philippines, but it sure doesn't feel like downtown San Francisco, only a few minutes walk away. Service in this cafeteria-style restaurant is both cheerful and helpful, and food choices are plentiful and cheap; with rotating daily specials all selling for less than $4.00. You want authentic Filipino food? Tuesday's specials include *dinuguan*--chocolate pork, and *callos*--tripe with garbanzos ($3.00). Or how about Friday, when one of the dishes of choice is *paksiw na pata*--pig's leg with banana flowers ($3.50).

Hours: M-F 11-3.
Cards: None.

## KOREAN RESTAURANT {Korea} (6/6=12)

3258 El Camino Real  Santa Clara  (408) 244-8531

    Surprisingly solicitous service and a few innovative surprises including gorgeous inlaid mother of pearl tables distinguish this from the spate of Peninsula Korean barbecue houses. A less ambitious menu than most Korean restaurants allows for the pursuit of a higher level of consistency and quality. Try *kal guk soo*--"handmade" noodle soup ($4.70), and *nagki hok kum*--octopus with hot sauce ($8.50). Although small and not glitzy, this is one of the area's better Korean restaurants.

Hours: Daily 10(a)-12(m).
Cards: V/MC/AE (over $20.00).

## MILVIA RESTAURANT {Korea} (6/6=12)

2237 Milvia St.  Berkeley  644-1343

    With brick walls and abstract paintings, the Milvia is among the most original of the Bay Area's numerous Korean establishments. Come to think of it, *Bronx-style* cheesecake and "*Uncle Fester's*" favorite ice cream dessert aren't standard fare on most local Korean menus either. Milvia's atmosphere is pleasant and its food is both good and eminently reasonable, with Korean favorites like *dak-gui* ($4.95) and *bi-bam-bap* ($5.25).

Hours: M-F 11:30-2:30; M-Sa 5-11.
Cards: V/MC.

## SEOUL GARDEN {Korea} (6/5=11)

22 Peace Plaza  San Francisco  563-7664

    Although still known as "Japantown", a number of Korean shops and restaurants--including Seoul Garden--now inhabit Peace Plaza and its environs. Seoul Garden is more ornate than the typical Korean barbecue house and offers a superb line of *hot pots* (boiling hot soups) including our favorite--*soft bean curd and clam* ($7.50). The Garden's pretty interior wood carving is nicely showcased by a rice paper skylight.

Hours: Daily 11(a)-12(m).
Cards: All major. No checks.

## INDONESIA {Indonesia} (4/6=10)

678 Post St.  San Francisco  474-4026

Possibly the most authentic of Bay Area Indonesian places--right down to the tacky newspaper cut outs touting it which are proudly taped to its window. Indonesia's food is plentiful and cheap (e.g. *nasi rames*--$3.95), but its menu is very limited. Don't expect to find specialty items here, particularly drinks. We asked to sample a beverage that people in Indonesia would drink, and were cheerfully handed a Coke. Dessert? A tropical fruit called *rambutan*--fresh from the can.

Hours: W-M 11:30-11.
Cards: V/MC.

## SEOUL HOUSE {Korea} (5/5=10)

348 13th St.  Oakland  893-7116

Seoul House boasts a nice handmade sign and door, but inside its atmosphere is quite ordinary, especially by Korean standards, since many Korean restaurant owners spend enormous sums on wood-carving and interior design. Prices are reasonable, though, especially at lunch when a large plate of *bi bim bap* sells for $4.95, and a tasty and equally filling bowl of *man du gook* goes for $4.75.

Hours: M-Sa 11-2; Th-Su 7(p)-2(a).
Cards: All major.

## CAFE GLENDA {The Philippines} (n/r)

1897 Solano Ave.  Berkeley  527-7499

Recently renovated, Cafe Glenda is prettier than it was, with a few Filipino ornaments overlooking what is still one of the most cramped restaurants in the area. Both times we've gone, however, at least two of the few authentic Filipino specials Glenda's offers (such as *adobo*) were not available, and service here has never been electrifying. Not enough Filipino goodness to warrant a special trip.

Hours: Tu-F 11:30-2; Tu-Su 5:30-10.
Cards: MC/V/AE.

## GOLDILOCKS {The Philippines} (n/r)

92 Serramonte Shopping Center  Daly City  992-2537

We are not given to singing the praises of fast food outlets, particularly when they are located on the food aisles of shopping malls. Goldilocks is a bit different, however. While the glorified stall has no atmosphere, the throng of Filipinos waiting patiently for "short orders" such as *pancit* or, more likely, homemade Filipino desserts such as *mamon*--sponge pastry ($.75), *rice pie* ($2.00) or *cassava root pie* ($2.75) attest to the fact that this is not your everyday fast food place.

Hours: Daily 11-9.
Cards: No.

## HAN IL KWAN {Korea} (n/r)

1802 Balboa Ave.  San Francisco  752-4447

This Korean barbecue house is distinguished only by some cheerful christmas lights, well placed mirrors and an imitation blue pagoda interior which gives the restaurant a festive feeling. It's always hard to rate the food in a Korean barbecue house since much of it you cook yourself; but the dishes we have had here (which you don't have to prepare) have been unspectacular.

Hours: Daily 10(a)-3(a).
Cards: V/MC. No checks.

## PAYUMO'S {The Philippines} (n/r)

53 Third St.  San Francisco  495-4440

In defiance of the adage that Filipino food must be cooked slowly, there are a burgeoning number of Filipino fast food restaurants. Payumo's, located in a nondescript "international" restaurant fair known as Yerba Buena Mall, is one of the better ones of this genre. Decent Filipino fare ranging from *tapas* to *diniguan* is served along with alternating daily specials. Prices are good too, but there's no Filipino atmosphere.

Hours: M-Sa 8:30-4:30.
Cards: No.

## KOREAN SECRET GARDEN {Korea} (n/r)

3430 El Camino Real   Santa Clara   (408) 244-5020

Pleasant but--as with many Korean restaurants--muzak is an instant negative. A few menu surprises including roast (actually broiled) herring ($8.50) and, for dessert, glazed sweet potatoes (at an expensive $4.95).

Hours: Daily 11-10.
Cards: V/MC. No checks.

## JAVA {Indonesia} (n/r)

417 Clement St.   San Francisco   752-1541

Although listed as Indonesian, the great majority of dishes Java serves are Chinese, and it is predominantly Chinese in decor. Still, there are enough Indonesian items to make up a rijstaffel, and Java *is* cheap.

Hours: W-M 11:30--11.
Cards: MC/V.

## JIN-GO-GAE {Korea} (n/r)

1330 Noriega St.   San Francisco   665-8548

A traditional Korean barbecue in a simple, but pleasant, atmosphere. Impressive lunch specials include bul go ki, kal bi, and j*ap chae bap*-- low calorie noodles with beef and vegetables ($5.50).

Hours: Daily 11:30-10:30.
Cards: V/MC.

## KOREAN RESTAURANT {Korea} (n/r)

2123 Irving St.   San Francisco   665-0966

One of the nicer new Korean barbecue houses around town. Try the barbecued salmon lunch special with vegetables and rice ($4.99).

Hours: Daily 10(a)-12(m).
Cards: All major (for orders over $20.00).

## CAFE ASTORIA {The Philippines} (n/r)

7367 Mission St. Daly City 991-9677

It seems to us that when we last visited two years ago both its cuisine and atmosphere were a little more Filipino. Now Astoria's ambience is virtually indistinguishable from that of a coffee house in Chinatown.

Hours: M-F 7(a)-3(p); Sa 7:30(a)-2(p).
Cards: No.

## OLIVER RITZ {The Philippines} (n/r)

6180-B Jarvis Ave. Newark 796-7617

"No shoes, no shirts, no service" we're used to. "No firearms allowed in restaurant" was a little new to us. The Ritz' only Filipino atmosphere is provided by the Filipino entertainers who perform nightly.

Hours: Su-Th 11(a)-12(m); F-Sa 11(a)-2(a).
Cards: V/MC.

## KOREA HOUSE {Korea} (n/r)

2340 El Camino Real Santa Clara (408) 249-0808

Korea House is a more attractive than average, but also more expensive, barbecue house which features good food and interesting desserts.

Hours: Su-M 10:30-10; Tu-Sa 10:30-3(a).
Cards: MC/V.

## DESSERT TRENDS {The Philippines} (n/r)

2232A Westborough Blvd. South San Francisco 589-1645

Many Filipino desserts and breakfasts including *tapsilog, tosilog* and *bangsilog*.

Hours: M-Sa 8:30-8; Su 8:30-7.
Cards: No.

## NOBLE PIES {Australia} (n/r)

5422 College Ave.   Oakland   653-2790

Nominally Aussie, Noble Pies does have an Australian owner and features a few Australian items like Aussie Meat Pie and Koala soda, but it's short on down-under atmosphere.

Hours: Daily 11-9.
Cards: No, but local checks accepted.

## KOREAN CORNER {Korea} (n/r)

340 University Ave.   Palo Alto   327-1357

This is Lora Kang's pleasant little shop in an international food fair in Palo Alto. It boasts no atmosphere whatsoever, but you'll like her *teriyaki chicken* and prices ($3.75-$5.50).

Hours: M-Sa 10-7.
Cards: No. Personal checks okay.

## FILIPINAS {The Philippines} (n/r)

953 Mission St.   San Francisco   543-0232

No Filipino atmosphere whatsoever, which is a shame because Filipinas' food is decent and cheap, and portions are enormous.

Hours: M-F 7(a)-6(p).
Cards: No.

## J & J PHILIPPINE CUISINE {The Philippines} (n/r)

905A E. Duane   Sunnyvale   732-6592

Authentic short order menu (pancit, adobo, lechon, etc.) in a typical, but not particularly exotic, red-checkered tablecloth atmosphere.

Hours: M-F 11-8:30; Sa 11-3.
Cards: None.

CENTRAL and SOUTH AMERICA

# 10. CENTRAL AND SOUTH AMERICA

*Brazil • Cuba • El Salvador • Haiti • Jamaica • Nicaragua • Peru • Puerto Rico*

To many Americans, three places best typify the romantic, exotic and carefree: South America, Central America and the Caribbean. In this chapter we will take a culinary expedition to each of these regions by visiting some of the best of their Bay Area representatives. For ease of reference, we will first discuss South American cuisine and culture. We will then continue on to our last two stops before heading home--Central America and the Caribbean.

## South America

### Argentina • Brazil • Peru

Recently, San Francisco lost "El Gaucho", its most prominent South American representative and the Bay Area's only purely Argentinian one. There remain, however, a couple of fine Brazilian restaurants, as well as an imposing and rapidly growing contingent of Peruvian ones. A few of the latter, most notably Berkeley's "Amaru", also offer some specialty dishes from other South American lands. So, while it may not be feasible to take a vicarious journey to every part of the continent without leaving the Bay Area, it is nevertheless possible to satiate one's craving for an exciting and romantic South American adventure.

### Tapas (*Entradas*--Appetizers)

Probably the best-loved South American appetizers are empanadas-- crunchy little turnovers similar to Indian *samosas*, but stuffed with different ingredients, such as olives and eggs. Empanadas are commonly associated with Argentina, but they are also extremely popular in Bolivia (where they are known as *saltenas*) and in other South American nations. In Brazil, for example, you are likely to be served *empadinhas de queijo*- -empanadas with cheese. Other popular Brazilian appetizers are *quibe*--a rolled ground beef and bulgur wheat mixture that bears more than a passing resemblance to Middle Eastern *kibbee*; *coxinha*--deep-fried chicken croquettes; *pastel*--a meat or cheese pastry not to be confused with the Puerto Rican cold meat hash of the same name; and *bolinho de bacalhau*--codfish croquette, a Portuguese colonial innovation.

Not to be outdone by its South American compatriots, Peru has concocted some interesting appetizers of its own including *papas a la huancaina*--an unusual combination of boiled potatoes and goat cheese; *anticuchos*--marinated beef hearts; and, above all perhaps, *ceviche*--a refreshing mix of fresh fish, chili and lime.

### *Platos Fuertes* (Main Courses)

Perhaps no nation has so exalted the status of beef as the Argentine, whose citizens, it is said, eat more of it than those of any other nation in the world. It is not surprising, therefore, that at Argentinian restaurants beef dishes such as *parrillada*--the traditional South American mixed grill featuring various cuts of beef, spiced sausages, and even some private parts--are the typical house specialties.

Brazilian entrees are more diverse, with a pronounced emphasis on dishes fashioned from either chicken, pork or seafood. Some of the best and most popular of these are *pernil de porco*--roast pork in wine sauce; *frango a brasileira*--chicken marinated in beer, then sauteed in cream; *muqueca de peixe*--fish, often red snapper, sauteed in coconut milk with shrimp and nuts; *xim xim de galinha*--chicken with shrimps and okra; and, of course, *feijoada*--smoked sausage and pork in black beans--the Brazilian national dish. Brazilian entrees will often be accompanied by either *tutu* and *farofa*. Both are side dishes made with fried yucca flour. The other ingredients in *tutu* are refried beans. In *farofa*, the flour is fried with olives, bacon and spices.

Some of Peru's best entrees are *bistek a la pobre*--a "*poor man's steak*", served with fried eggs and bananas; *lomo saltado*--beef strips with vegetables and chili; *chupe de camarones*--a rich seafood soup made with green peas, eggs, potatoes, prawns and corn; and *cau cau*--tripe. Specialty dishes from other South American nations you may occasionally encounter are *pabellon criollo*--Venezuelan brisket of beef in tomato sauce, sometimes served with *caraotas*--black beans; *picante de pollo*--a spicy chicken dish from Bolivia; and *curanto*--Chilean bouillabaisse.

## *Bebidas* (Drinks) and Postres *(Sobremesas*--Desserts*)*

In addition to South American wines and beers, of which there are many including *xingu*--Brazilian black beer; there are a few non-alcoholic South American drinks worth getting to know. Chief among these are *guarana*--a Brazilian soft drink made from a tropical fruit of the same name, *inka cola*--a popular Peruvian soft drink which tastes a bit like bubble gum, and *chicha morada*--a tasty Peruvian thirst-quencher derived from a tropical South American bean.

Although almost always available at Peruvian restaurants, for some reason alfajores--homemade coconut butter cookies--seldom appear on their menus. When made right, "alfajores" may be among the world's most tempting cookies. Other interesting South American sweets include three from Brazil: *pudim de coco*--coconut pudding, *carioca*--guava and ice cream, and *quindim*--a coconut cupcake; as well as *arroz con leche*--rice pudding, from all over South America, via Spain.

## AMARU (Peru) (8/10=18)

2037 Shattuck Ave.   Berkeley   549-7075

It isn't hard to figure out what makes Amaru special. Fresh flowers in ceramic vases, a solitary string of white lights, hanging strands of fresh garlic, flags depicting each of the countries represented on the restaurant's ample bill of fare--all combine to imbue Amaru with ambience aplenty. For quality South American cuisine in a relaxed, even romantic setting, Amaru is hard to beat. Amaru's *tapas* (appetizers) are all very good, especially *papas a la huancaina*--potatoes in cheese sauce ($3.75), and ceviche--sliced fish marinated in lime, chili, onions and fresh herbs. But some of its entrees are simply extraordinary. Take *ajo de gallina*--chicken strips sauteed in a spicy sauce of cheese, annatto oil and walnuts ($11.95). This native Peruvian dish--served with egg, olives and boiled potatoes--is one of the most innovative and delightful poultry courses you'll find anywhere. Amaru also serves several dishes from other South American countries that are well worth a try, including such finds as the Brazilian creole dish *vatapa--mixed fish and seafood in a spicy sauce made from peanuts, coconut milk, ginger, cilantro and peppers ($14.50);* curanto--a Chilean dish featuring mixed fish, shellfish, chicken and sausages in a wine and pepper sauce ($16.50); and *pabellon criollo*--Venezuelan brisket of beef topped with a tomato and onion sauce and served with *caraotas--*Venezuelan black beans ($12.75). For dessert, we suggest you pass on the interesting-sounding, but bland, Chilean pastry *torta milhojas*--made with sweet cream, orange, almonds and liqueur ($3.95)--in favor of Amaru's superb *alfajores*--Peruvian butter cookies made with sweet cream and coconut ($2.00), or arroz con leche--creamy spiced rice pudding ($1.75). Only two things prevent Amaru from fulfilling its true potential. The first is erratic, at times even reluctant, service. The second is that by offering, in addition to Peruvian specialties, dishes from almost every other South American country and even several from Spain, Amaru's chef may be a bit overextended. While quite a few of Amaru's South American items are superb, you can obtain better versions of some of its Spanish specialties elsewhere, at restaurants which concentrate on Spanish fare. Therefore, though you may be sorely tempted by such classic Spanish offerings as *calamares al ajillo*--prawns in garlic sauce ($13.50), *paella* (marinera--$15.95 or Valenciana--$16.95), and flan ($2.95)--we recommend that you stick to Amaru's tantalizing South American slate, and particularly to the Peruvian dishes at which Amaru excels.

Hours: Tu-Sa  5:30--10; Su 5--9.
Cards: V/MC/AE.

## EUNICE'S {Brazil} (8/8=16)

3392 24th St.   San Francisco   821-4600

A festive atmosphere, twinkling lights, colorful photographs--mostly of Carnaval--fresh flowers and always lively Brazilian music greet you at Eunice's, Northern California's premier Brazilian restaurant. Perhaps the restaurant's colorful place mats say it best: "live one day at a time and make it a masterpiece". Foodwise, Eunice's takes it own advice, creating a number of masterpieces on plates. While head chef for a wealthy Brazilian industrialist, the restaurant's chef/proprietor cooked for the likes of Robert Kennedy and Ronald Reagan. Now, such delightful indigenous dishes as *camarao a balana*--shrimp steamed in coconut milk ($8.95); *muqueca de peixe a capixaba*--spicy red snapper and tomatoes ($10.95); and *mariscada meierles*--fish and shellfish in white wine ($11.95) can be all yours. Although the emphasis at Eunice's is on fish and seafood, other dishes such as *pernil assado*--roasted pork with collard greens and black beans) are served, and Eunice's *feijoada* is undoubtedly the best around.

Hours: Tu-Sa 5-10.
Cards: All major.

## FINA ESTAMPA {Peru} (6/9=15)

2374 Mission St.   San Francisco   824-4437

Darkwook panels, a coat of arms and other Spanish paraphernalia beckon you into this, the newest and best of San Francisco's cache of fine Peruvian restaurants. We must admit that, when we first saw Fina's menu, we were somewhat skeptical about an Inner Mission restaurant charging $8.00--$10.00 for a la carte lunches. But by the time we got around to paying a visit, a large throng of contented-looking visitors were already busy wolfing down Fina's food. No wonder. Some of Fina's traditional Peruvian dishes, such as *bistek a la pobre,* are splendid. While others, like *chicken aji panca*--made with the same Peruvian hot sauce used to flavor *anticuchos*--are not as good, they are still innovative and tasty. Fina Estampa also serves some delightful side dishes like chilled hominy; and, as an alternative to the common Peruvian dessert *alfajores*--coconut butter cookies, it offers *mazamorra morada*--a fascinating concoction made from the same bean as the popular Peruvian drink *chicha morada.*

Hours: Daily 11:30-10.
Cards: All major.

## DE PAULA'S {Brazil} (7/8=15)

2114 Fillmore St.   San Francisco   346-9888

Not many restaurants flaunt their ethnic character like De Paula's. Although, from the outside, modern and nondescript; inside (imitation) parrots swing from the rafters, Indian headdresses line the walls, and plants and fresh flowers abound. It is always a pleasure to step in from the Fillmore to one of those insistent samba rhythms which perpetually play on De Paula's stereo. De Paula's menu is also refreshingly authentic, with appetizers like *bacalhau*--codfish (a staple of both Brazil and its former colonial master, Portugal--$1.50); *coxinha*--chicken croquette ($1.60); and *empadinhas* ($1.60), Brazil's answer to the Argentinian *empandada*. Although De Paula's places an unfortunate emphasis on pizza, it also serves a couple of authentic Brazilian lunch specials daily. We recommend that you go on Friday, when *feijoada*--a spicy black bean and pork stew, Brazil's national dish, is served. Authentic and tasty Brazilian sweets are also offered, including *quindim*--egg yolk with coconut cream ($2.00).

Hours: M-F 11:30--2:30; Su-Th 5-11; F-Sa 5-12.
Cards: All major.

## EL TUMI {Peru} (6/6=12)

3748 San Pablo Dam Rd.   El Sobrante   222-0607

While predominately Peruvian, with simple red tablecloths and a few fabric wall hangings of Inca design, El Tumi also serves a host of Mexican meals. In trying to do Mexican as well as Peruvian, El Tumi spreads itself a little thin. Indeed, during the week, El Tumi features only 4 authentic Peruvian dishes--such as *lomito soldado* and *camarones rancheros*--as compared to 17 Mexican ones. It is on weekends that El Tumi's true Peruvian colors show. That is when a host of other Peruvian specialties like *escabeche de pollo--fried chicken with boiled eggs, onions and potatoes*-- are brought out. Neither its *papas a la huancaina* nor *escabeche* are particularly good, and the *pescado ahogado* (drowned fish) might be better called *pescado aburrido* (boring fish), because it is so bland; but some of El Tumi's Peruvian meat dishes, like *bistek a la pobre*, are solid. Live music is featured after 9 p.m. on weekends but, by then, El Tumi is very crowded. Besides, the music isn't Peruvian either.

Hours: Daily 11-11.
Cards: No.

## ALEJANDRO'S {Peru} (6/6=12)

1840 Clement St. San Francisco 668-1184

This pretty, fashionable, but somewhat expensive restaurant probably should rate higher. However, since it is so eclectic, featuring Mexican and Spanish dishes as well as Peruvian ones--it is difficult to get a true sense of where Alejandro's loyalties lie. It does boast what is probably the finest selection of *tapas* in Northern California (despite a recent challenge by El Oso), and the *zarzuela* and *paella Valenciana* (both Spanish dishes) are particularly good here. Price range for Peruvian dishes--$13.00-$16.00.

Hours: M-Th 5-11; F-Sa 5-12(m); Su 4-11.
Cards: All major.

## FRANCESCA'S {Peru} (6/7=13)

2909 Mission St. San Francisco 648-3368

Ceiling fans reminiscent of "Dark Passages" and a room-size seaview mural dominate this happy red-brick Peruvian restaurant in the heart of San Francisco's Mission District. The best time to come is on weekends when a special Peruvian breakfast is served. Francesca's regular menu features traditional Peruvian specialties like *lomo saltido* and *picante*--a delicious but spicy mixed seafood combination ($8.50).

Hours: Daily 11(a)-9.
Cards: No.

## DON QUIXOTE {Peru} (6/6=12)

2351 Mission St. San Francisco 550-8325

Inviting wrought iron gates open to this simple but pleasant "international"--but primarily Peruvian--hacienda. Its primarily Latin clientele, and the fact that you need to speak Spanish to order, mark this as an authentic stop. While Don Quixote's menu is not totally Peruvian, there are enough Peruvian specials, like *arroz chaufa*--a Peruvian-style seafood combination ($8.25), to warrant the trip.

Hours: Daily 12(n)-8.
Cards: No.

## TAMBO CAFE {Peru} (6/6=12)

1981 Shattuck Ave.   Berkeley   841-6884

This relatively new place has an effervescent atmosphere highlighted by friendly service and typically cheerful and loud Andean music. Tambo doesn't have much in the way of food--only half a dozen entrees and a couple of desserts--but what it does serve is well made and very cheap (e.g. *causa*, with *atun*--tuna, or *pollo*--chicken ($2.25) and *alfajores*-- classic Peruvian coconut butter cookies ($.60).

Hours: M-Sa 11-10.
Cards: No, but they sometimes take checks.

## NINO'S {Brazil} (n/r)

1916 Martin Luther King Way   Berkeley   845-9303

Decent Brazilian atmosphere and lively, authentic music on compact disks are offset by the an overemphasis on pizza and sandwiches--almost to the exclusion of an otherwise authentic slate of such interesting Brazilian dishes as *vatapa*, *moranga* and *muqueca de camarao* ($7.95-$9.95). A change of ownership in December, 1988--together with a fairly recent menu change (July, 1989)--may portend better times ahead.

Hours: Daily 11-11.
Cards: V\MC

## CIPRIANI'S {Peru} (n/r)

3515 Mission St.   San Francisco   550-9288

Since we last visited in July 1989, Cipriani's telephone has been disconnected, portending probably doom. We were unable to confirm this at press time however. Of Cipriani's we had written: "there are some touches we could do without (such as a prominent solicitation of "housewives" to register for a chance to win an "Oneida meat cleaver"), but the overall effect is cheerful and genuine." We'll let you know.

Hours: N.A. See above.
Cards: All major.

# CENTRAL AMERICA & THE CARIBBEAN

Cuba • El Salvador • Haiti • Jamaica • Nicaragua • Puerto Rico

With all the one way traffic from Central America to Northern California in recent years, you would have to figure that the Bay Area would have some pretty good Central American restaurants, and it does. Surprisingly, however, virtually all of these represent only two countries--Nicaragua and El Salvador. Salvadorean restaurants tend to place heavy emphasis on Mexican food. Indeed, many offer more Mexican dishes than Salvadorean ones. The chief exception is that virtually all Salvadorean restaurants serve *pupusas*--thick doughy pies, usually stuffed with cheese. Nicaraguan menus are a bit more innovative, with specialties like *baho*--steamed beef with yuccas and bananas; and original desserts such as *pio quinto*--rum cake with custard, and *bunuelos*--yucca fritters with honey.

Although Cuba would surely argue the point, Jamaica may boast the definitive Caribbean cuisine. There are many superb Jamaican dishes, drinks and desserts you will want to try. Start with *jerk* pork, jerk chicken or--for that matter--jerk anything. "Jerking" is a Jamaican method of food preparation in which the meat or fish is seasoned with Jamaican pimento berries, then slowly baked outdoors over a pit until it is infused with a tangy, smoked taste. Other Jamaican specialty dishes include *curried goat, and ackee and saltfish*--Jamaica's national dish made from spicy salted cod and *ackee*--an unusual native vegetable. One of our favorite liqueurs, *pimento*, is also from Jamaica.

Three Cuban dishes are especially appealing: *ropa vieja*--shredded beef with peppers; *sandwich a la Cubane*--the famed Cuban sandwich made from ham, cheese and pork; and *piccadillo*--a wonderful ground beef hash. Other Cuban offerings include *camarones empanizados*--fried breaded shhrimps, and *rabo encendido*--Cuban-style oxtail soup. Some Cuban side orders of note include *yuca*--fried yucca; *mofongo*--crushed plantains; and, of course, *frijoles negros*--the infamous Cuban black beans. Although *flan* may be Cuba's most popular dessert, *cascos de guayabas*--guava shells with cream cheese--may be its best.

## LA BELLE CREOLE {Haiti} (10/10=20)

4090 San Pablo Ave.  Emeryville  654-6008

The only Haitian restaurant in the Bay Area, this unique jewel is one of our favorite places in the East Bay and--until now at least--one of our best kept secrets. From the standpoint of decor alone La Belle Creole--with its gorgeous one-of-a-kind lamps and attractive Caribbean paintings--could justify its "10" rating for atmosphere. But what most attracts about the atmosphere of La Belle Creole are the intangible elements provided by owner and master chef Gerard Noel--such as extraordinary service, genuine concern that you enjoy your meal, and--oh yes--phenomenal French Caribbean food at surprisingly affordable prices. This isn't the kind of place that you can just walk into anytime you want and expect to order whatever you'd like. Not only are reservations required, they are requested at least *a day* in advance. Further, at the time you reserve, you are expected to place your order. Decide what you want for dinner a day in advance? A bit inconvenient, but not an arbitrary formality. Gerard needs the time to purchase what you desire and make sure that it will be ready to prepare when you arrive. Why, you say, would he have to individually purchase your order? Simple, not too many places go through sufficient quantities of items such as *African Guinea hen*, pheasant, conch and roast goat to justify keeping a fresh supply on hand. You say that conch and pheasant aren't special enough for you? Then how about alligator (it tastes a little like filet mignon). Or try any one of the restaurants more traditional creole specialties such as *Le Gumbo aux Calaloux des Caraibes*--Caribbean-style gumbo with chicken, shrimp, sausage, crab and okra; *or le lamby a l'aubergine saupoudree de fromage*--conch sauteed in spiced butter sauce, mixed with spiced eggplant and grated cheese. Other specialty items include *le lapin au petits pois sauciere et aux onions*--marinated rabbit with shallots, onions, peas, nuts and raisins in a brown mushroom sauce; as well as less exotic dishes like poached salmon and filet mignon. With all meals, a special Caribbean style vegetable soup, fried plantains, and an exquisite side of rice and beans flavored with coconut is served. Still, prices at La Belle Creole are only in the $12.00-$14.00 range. Possibly the only downside is that the Emeryville neighborhood in which La Belle Creole is set looks a little tough; but everybody has been friendly to us, and places like this just--in any location--don't come along every day.

Hours: Tu-Sa 5:30-9:30. Other days "on request".
Cards: No. But personal checks are accepted.

## EL CUBANE {Cuba} (7/9=16)

1432 Valencia St. San Francisco 824-6655

Financial District folks rarely venture far out to lunch which is a shame because, only a few minutes and $.80 (by BART) away, an entirely different and infinitely more relaxing world is waiting in the Mission District, with its scores of Latin American restaurants. Among these are a handful of Cuban places, the best of which is El Cubane--a spacious and cheerful haunt only two blocks from the 24th Street Bart Station. At El Cubane, white cane furniture and potted plants help capture the carefree spirit of the Caribbean without conveying the feeling that the proprietors don't care about the quality of their food. Our favorite of a host of outrageously underpriced lunch specials is *piccadillo criollo*--a spicy ground beef hash served with fried eggs on top, *frijoles negros* (black beans) and rice ($3.99). Dinner entrees cost more, but are still quite reasonable. Try *chilindron de chivo*--goat stew ($7.50). Best dessert: *cascos de guayaba*--cheese in guava shells ($1.50), a real Caribbean treat.

Hours: 12(n)-10.
Cards: All major

## CUBAN INTERNATIONAL {Cuba} (8/8=16)

625 N. Sixth St. San Jose (408) 288-6783

One flight up (and several time zones away) lies Cuba International, a refreshing Cuban/Puerto Rican hybrid in downtown San Jose. As with many Caribbean representatives, at Cuba International you have to think to figure out what makes the restaurant seem so different from, say, the run of the mill Mexican places which dot the Bay. Ceiling fans and little Cuban pictures and posters are a start. Lively conversation in thickly accented Spanish with a backdrop of pounding Caribbean music also help. But, whatever it is that evokes images of Jimmy Buffet changing attitudes and latitudes and pre-Fidel movies about the good life in Havana, you're sure to like it. Hey, don't get us wrong, with no floor show and fake flowers, the Copacabana this isn't. But prices aren't high, its food is pretty good, especially soups like *fabada*--white bean ($4.25); Caribbean lunch specials like *tamal Cubano* and Puerto Rican *pastel*--shredded beef pie (both $4.50); and *moros y cristianos* (translated as Cuban rice--$2.25).

Hours: Daily 10:45-9.
Cards: V/MC.

## NICARAGUA {Nicaragua} (7/6=13)

3015 Mission St. San Francisco 826-3672

    Nicaragua's humdrum atmosphere--wood panelling lined with framed tourist posters and a map of Nicaragua--is considerably enlivened by cheerful, efficient service and zippy Spanish conversation. You get the feeling that the customers are there almost as much for the conversation as for the food. But Nicaragua's authentic fare is worth a visit by itself. For a traditional Nicaraguan dish, we favor *baho*--steamed beef, yucca and bananas ($6.50), and *tajadas*--sliced bananas with beans and sour cream ($3.75). Other traditional offerings include *vigoron*--pork rinds and yucca ($3.99), and *sopa albondigas*--meat ball soup ($3.50). Portions tend to be large--so large in fact that many of the already reasonably priced items are available as *media ordenes*--half orders--a nice feature for those who want to experiment with more than one dish. When available, desserts at Nicaragua are a real delight, particularly *cajeta de leche*--milk fudge ($1.00), and *sopa borracha* (literally "drunken soup"--a rum cake).

Hours: Daily 11-9:45.
Cards: None.

## LAS TINAJAS {Nicaragua} (7/6=13)

2338 Mission St. San Francisco 695-9933

    A modern, lively and spacious cafeteria-style Nicaraguan restaurant, Las Tinajas--with nice paintings and pleasant pink tablecloths--is not your typical Mission District restaurant. Still, the production line manner in which food may stand for hours is not calculated to bring out the best in either atmosphere or cuisine. Las Tinajas offers three lunch specials daily. The best days to come are Tuesday and Friday. On both days, traditional Nicaraguan *baho*--steamed beef with yucca and banana ($5.25) is served. On Tuesday, you can also obtain a healthy portion of tasty *salpicon*--minced meat hash ($4.95). A number of interesting fish and prawn dishes are also available; and Tinajas' vegetable plate--fried cheese and *gallo y pinto* (rice and beans--$4.95) is both good and a good deal. All portions at Las Tinajas range from large to huge. The restaurant's best dessert, *sopa borracha* ($1.00), is good but would be better if it wasn't served in a plastic container.

Hours: M-Th 11:30-6:30; F-Sa 11:30-7:30.
Cards: All major.

## EL NUEVO FRUTILANDIA CAFE {Cuba} (6/7=13)

3077 24th St.  San Francisco  648-2958

Nuevo Frutilandia is a small, pleasant place which--depending on how you look at it--is either a Puerto Rican cafe or a Cuban diner. Foods from both countries are showcased, as well as maps, pictures and flags. Some seafood dishes are offered but the choices are mostly meat. Try the *ropa vieja*--shredded beef with peppers ($6.50), a Cuban specialty, with a side order of *mofongo*--crushed plantains in garlic. The best reason for going, however, is *mamey*--a Cuban tropical fruit shake--$2.00).

Hours: M-W 11:30-9; Th-Su 11:30-9:30.
Cards: No. Personal checks accepted.

## CUBA RESTAURANT {Cuba} (5/7=12)

2886 16th St.  San Francisco  864-9871

Far from extraordinary, Cuba nevertheless has pleasant atmosphere and offers Bay Area restaurant-goers the opportunity to experience some interesting examples of Cuban cuisine, and even one Bolivian dish, *lobo montado*--sirloin steak with fried eggs on top. Also interesting: *potage de garbanzo*--chickpea soup ($3.50) and *pescado entomado*--sea bass sauteed with tomatoes is a white wine sauce ($8.95).

Hours: M-F 11-10; Sa-Su 12(n)-10.
Cards: All major.

## LAS PALMERAS {El Salvador} (5/6=11)

2721 Mission St.  San Francisco  285-7796

Las Palmeras offers a few indigenous Salvadorean dishes like *pupusas de queso* ($1.00 each), as well as a host of Mexican ones. The food is a good value, and there are some very interesting dishes, although we're not too sure about all the items featuring pig organs (ears, heart, etc.); and the pinatas and map of Mexico detract from Las Palmeras otherwise authentic Central American feel.

Hours: M-Th 8(a)-10(p); F-Su 8(a)-11.
Cards: No. Travelers checks accepted.

## LA SANTANECA DE LA MISSION {Salvador} (n/r)

2815 Mission St.  San Francisco  285-2131

A typical but pleasant Salvadorean restaurant with numerous posters of El Salvador as well as some incongruous German beer advertisements, posters and steins. As with most Salvadorean places, too many Mexican dishes are served, but La Sanateca de la Mission also features a number of authentic Salvadorean ones including *lengua en salsa*--beef tongue in a spicy sauce ($5.25), *carne adobada*--seasoned pork steak ($5.75), and *carne deshilchada*--spicy beef, eggs, onions and tomatoes ($5.50).

Hours: M-Th 11:30-8; F-Su 11:30-9.
Cards: No.

## WELCOME MAT {Caribbean} (n/r)

807 Valencia St.  San Francisco  647-3663

The Welcome Mat is eclectic. Not only does it feature specialties from each of the primary Caribbean Islands (Jamaica, Cuba and Puerto Rico), but from such places as Dominica, Martinique and Trinidad as well. The Welcome Mat even serves Jamaican *jerk chicken*, although it's not terribly authentic. Nice Caribbean music compliments fairly attractive surroundings with small paintings, Haitian dolls and lots and lots of wicker.

Hours: Tu-Sa 6(p)-12(m).
Cards: MC/V.

## EL AMANACER {El Salvador} (n/r)

1183 Portrero Ave.  San Francisco  282-2110

One of the area's more ornate Central American restaurants, El Amanacer displays an abundance of pictures and photographs, mainly of El Salvador. Black wrought iron, chandeliers, plants and (imitation) parrots also contribute to a somewhat Central American feeling. El Amancer's food is decent, but the emphasis here, as at most Salvadorean restaurants, is on Mexican food.

Hours: Daily 11:30-11.
Cards: None.

## JOSE'S PIZZA AND RESTAURANT {Cuba} (n/r)

2275 El Camino Real  Palo Alto  853-9642

A "Cuban" restaurant with few Cuban amenities, Jose's specializes in Argentinian sour dough pizza and *empanadas*. Interesting but not particularly authentic atmosphere. Good but not particularly authentic food.

Hours: Tu-F 11:30-2; Tu-Th 5:30-9; F-Su 5:30-9:30.
Cards: All major.

## ENSENADA {El Salvador} (n/r)

2976 Mission St.  San Francisco  826-4160

Although Salvadorean *pupusas* (cheese pies) are a house specialty, the primary emphasis is on Mexican dishes. Food and prices are good, however, and Ensenada is a stone's throw from the 24th Street Bart.

Hours: W-F 11:30-9:30; Sa-Su 11:30-12:30 (a).
Cards: V/MC.

## CARMEN & FAMILY BAR-B-QUE {Jamaica} (n/r)

3250 Adeline St.  Berkeley  652-7427

Very little Jamaican at this "Jamaican barbecue" restaurant, and the service can be downright bizarre.

Hours: Daily 11:30-9.
Cards: V/MC.

# APPENDIX A--RESTAURANTS NOT REVIEWED

**BASQUE:**
    Basque Hotel and Restaurant
    15 Romolo Pl.  San Francisco  398-1359

    Cafe Villa Basque
    1600 Lincoln Ave.  San Rafael  459-6161

    Guernica
    2009 Bridgeway  Sausalito  332-1512

    Obrero Hotel & Basque Restaurant
    1208 Stockton St.  San Francisco  989-3960

**BURMESE:**
    Burma House
    720 Post St.  San Francisco  775-1156

**CAMBODIAN:**
    Angkor Wat Cambodian Restaurant
    4217 Geary Blvd.  San Francisco  221-7887

    Cambodian House Restaurant
    5625 Geary Blvd.  San Francisco  668-5888

**CARIBBEAN:**
    Cha Cha Cha Cafe
    1805 Haight St.  San Francisco  386-5758

    Geva's
    482 Hayes St.  San Francisco  863-1220

**CUBAN:**
    Catalina's
    891 Island Dr.  Alameda  521-4032

**CZECH:**
    Golden Duck Grill
    2953 Baker St.  San Francisco  922-7144

Heart of Europe (Also German)
685 Sutter St. San Francisco 441-5678

**DANISH:**

Einer's
1901 Clement St. San Francisco 386-9860

Little Copenhagen
2826 El Camino Real  Redwood City 356-6616

**ENGLISH:**

Agatha's English Tea Room
1475 Burlingame Ave. Burlingame 348-8341

Bit of England
1448 Burlingame Ave. Burlingame 344-1540

Britania Arms of Almaden
5027 Almaden Expressway (408) 266-0550

Britannia Arms Pub
1087 S. Saratoga-Snyvale Rd. San Jose (408) 252-7262

Duke of Edinburgh
10801 N. Wolfe Road Cupertino (408) 446-3853

Henry VIII
673 Geary Blvd. San Francisco 775-5258

Liverpool Lil's
2942 Lyon San Francisco 921-6664

Village Green English Restaurant
89 Portola Ave. El Granada 726-3690

Wild Strawberry
929-B Edgewater Blvd. Foster City 377-1989

**ETHIOPIAN:**

Asmara
5020 Telegraph Ave. Oakland 547-5100

Massawa
1538 Haight St. San Francisco 621-4129

**FILIPINO:**

Gold Ribbon Bake Shop & Restaurant
380 S. Main St.   Milpitas   (408) 942-0661

Mabuhay House of Seafood
6045 Mission St.   Daly City   587-7666

Mamonluk
2025 Gellert Blvd.   Daly City   878-5612

Manila Bay
1230 El Camino Real   San Bruno   742-9588

Manila Express
425 Gellert Blvd.   Daly City   878-8158

Max's Fried Chicken
2239 Gellert Blvd.   South San Francisco   878-0610

Mister Go
1710 Berryessa Rd.   San Jose   (408) 729-6950

Nayang Filipino
13876 Doolittle Dr.   San Leandro   895-2433

Pacific Breeze
3016 E. 14th   Oakland   535-1820

Philippine Gourmet
1770 Clear Lake Ave.   Milpitas   (408) 946-1566

Sinugba Seafood Restaurant
2055 Gellert Blvd.--#5   Daly City   878-1826

Sulo Filipino Coffee Shop
1518 Webster St.   Alameda   865-7889

Sweet Sensations Bake Shop & Fast Food
31861 Alvarado Blvd.   Union City   489-5890

**GERMAN:**

Beethoven
1701 Powell St.   San Francisco   391-4488

Buckeye
Highway 101   Mill Valley   332-1292

Gasthaus Zum Goldener Adler
1380 S. Main   Milpitas   (408) 946-6141

Little Bavaria
5611 Redwood Hwy.   Novato   883-7334

Pacific Sunset
2650 Judah   San Francisco   661-4465

Sea Cliff
1801 Clement St.   San Francisco   386-6266

**GREEK:**

Demitri's Deli
174 E. 3rd Ave.   San Mateo   340-9242

El Greco
11891 Dublin Blvd.   Dublin   828-1154

Greco-Romana Pizzeria
2448 Clement St.   San Francisco   387-0626

Greek Islands Delights (The)
2218 San Mateo Fashion Island   San Mateo   341-3383

Niki's Greek Restaurant
2785 Castro Valley Blvd.   Castro Valley   582-5864

Seven Ports
1088 Shell Blvd.   Foster City   345-3010

Taverna Athena
201 Broadway   Oakland   893-6000

**HUNGARIAN:**

The Hungarian Restaurant
1201 Laurel St.   San Carlos   594-9170

**INDIAN:**

Angaare
34579 Alvarado-Niles Road   Union City   487-6112

Cafe India
1521 Main St.   Walnut Creek   944-5403

Chandni
2288 Lincoln Ave.   San Jose   (408) 723-0219

Embassy
1160 Burlingame Ave.  Burlingame  348-5555

Gita's
Three Embarcadero Center  San Francisco  864-4306

India Mahal
3790 Mowry Ave.  Fremont  793-7551

India Oven
237 Fillmore St.  San Francisco  626-1628

Kabab Cafe
2634 Alum Rock Ave.  San Jose  (408) 929-5117

Kabila
29286 Union City Blvd.  471-6666

Khyber India
846 Jefferson Ave.  Redwood City  369-4522

Mela
417 O'Farrell St.  San Francisco  776-7171

Mumtaj
126 Castro St.  Mountain View  961-2433

New Delhi
160 Ellis St.  San Francisco  397-8470

Nusrat Sweets
146 George St.  San Jose  (408) 293-8832

Royal Taj
5155 Stevens Creek Blvd  (408) 248-1365

Royal Taj
1350 Campbell Ave.  Campbell  (408) 559-6801

Sabina
4607 Clayton Road  Concord  827-9112

Shish Mahal
1991B Santa Rita Road  Pleasanton  484-2850

Taste of India
5144 Mowry Ave.  Fremont  791-1316

**INDONESIAN:**
Ori-Deli
5479 Snell Ave.    San Jose    (408) 578-6262

**IRISH:**
Finn McCool's
10905 N. Wolfe Road   Cupertino   (408) 253-7111

**JAMAICAN:**
Prince Neville Jamaican Restaurant
1279 Fulton St.   San Francisco   861-9433

**KOREAN:**
Cherryland Cafe
22472 Meekland Ave.   Hayward   582-8448

Korea House
1640 Post St.   San Francisco   563-1388

Korean Bar-B-Que
1610 El Camino Real   San Bruno   583-0702

Korean Palace
2297 Stevens Creek Blvd.   San Jose   (408) 279-9686

Palace Korean Restaurant & Night Club
1205 The Alameda   San Jose   (408) 275-9869

Sam Da Do
937 Geary Blvd.   San Francisco   771-1877

Seoul Restaurant
138 S. Main St.   Milpitas   (408) 946-5446

**MALAYSIAN:**
Satay House
1818 Tully Road   San Jose   (408) 238-8804

**MIDDLE EAST:**
Grapeleaf (The)
4031 Balboa   San Francisco   668-1515

Habibi
3906 Washington Blvd.   Fremont   659-9600

Jawad Cafe & Deli
1799 McAlister St.   San Francisco   921-1237

Orient Express
50 Steuart St.   San Francisco   957-1776

Pasha
1516 Broadway   San Francisco   885-4477

Sultan (The)
3099 El Camino Real   Santa Clara   (408) 296-0451

**MOROCCAN:**
El Mansour
3123 Clement St.   San Francisco   751-2312

Mamounia
4411 Balboa   San Francisco   752-6566

Marrakech Palace
419 O'Farrell St.   San Francisco   776-6717

Menara
41 E. Gish Road   San Jose   (408) 453-1983

Royal Morocco
14510 Big Basin Way   Saratoga   (408) 741-0224

**NICARAGUAN:**
Las Cazuelas
6123 Mission St.   Daly City   826-3672

Red Balloon
2763 Mission St.   San Francisco   285-1749

**PERSIAN:**
Bay Bistro
43 South B St.   San Mateo   347-8686

Casablanca
979 San Pablo Ave.   Albany   525-2000

Caspian
1063 E. El Camino Real   Sunnyvale   (408) 248-6332

Chatanoga
2725 El Camino Real   Santa Clara   (408) 241-1200

European Deli and Hastou Bakery
1500 Monument Blvd.   Concord   689-1011

Kabab House
1300 Galindo   Concord   671-0969

Manssur's
801 W. Hamilton Ave.   Campbell   (408) 866-1588

Norman's Restaurant
4949 Stevenson Blvd.   Fremont   656-1398

Paradise
1350 Grant Rd.   Mountain View   968-5949

Pars Restaurant
352 El Camino Real   San Bruno   871-5151

Pit Cozy
22343 Redwood Road   Castro Valley   581-4499

Teasara Cafe and Restaurant
1138 Sartoga Ave.   San Jose   (408) 241-5115

**RUSSIAN:**

Misha's Russian Cafe
21 Tamalpais Ave   San Anselmo   456-9825

**SALVADOR:**

Los Cocos Salvadorian Restaurant
1449 Fruitvale Ave.   Oakland   536-3079

**SPANISH:**

La Bodega
1337 Grant Ave.   San Francisco   433-0439

La Roca
4288 24th St.   San Francisco   282-7780

Little Spain
1333 Columbus Ave.   San Francisco   673-3273

Tango Cafe & Restaurant
1232 4th St.   San Rafael   459-2721

**SRI LANKAN:**

Curry Village (The)
1187-A S. Saratoga-Snyvale Rd.   San Jose   (408) 973-9960

**SWEDISH:**

Scandinavian Delicatessen
2251 Market St. San Francisco 861-9913

Swedish Place (The)
824 E. St. San Rafael 453-9481

Swedish Place (The)
Hwy 1 (2mi So. of) Half Moon Bay 726-7322

**SWISS:**

Alpenrose
13100 Skyline Bl. Woodside 851--1136

Alpine Inn (The)
401 Primrose Road Burlingame 347-5733

Alps (The)
5200 Mowry Ave. Fremont 791-1141

Lucerne
416 San Mateo Ave. San Bruno 871-9895

Luzern
1427 Noriega San Francisco 664-2353

Swiss Alps
605 Post St. San Francisco 885-0947

# APPENDIX B--GLOSSARY OF ETHNIC FOODS

**abesh** *(Ethiopia)*--the Ethiopian equivalent of fenugreek.
**acar campur** *(Indonesia)*--pickled vegetable salad.
**achaar** *(India)*--mango pickle.
**ackee** *(Jamaica)*--a Jamaican vegetable, often eaten with salted codfish.
**adobo** *(The Philippines)*--meat (usually pork or chicken) in a sour sauce.
**agar-agar** *(Indonesia)*--a dessert similar to jello.
**akbar mashti** *(Persia)*--honey ice cream.
**alfajores** *(Peru)*--coconut butter cookies.
**almejas** *(Spain)*--clams, usually served in ajo *(garlic)*.
**aloo tikki** *(India)*--fried potato patties stuffed with spiced lentils.
**aloo chat** *(India)*--a cold spicy combination of potatoes and vegetables.
**aloo gobi** *(India)*--cauliflower and potatoes cooked with herbs and spices.
**anticuchos** *(Peru)*--marinated beef hearts.
**apritadang manok** *(The Philippines)*--chicken stew.
**arnab** *(Middle East)*--braised rabbit in paprika sauce.
**arni pisto** *(Greece)*--roast leg of lamb with garlic and lemon.
**arroz caldo** *(The Philippines)*--rice porridge.
**arroz con leche** *(Spain/South America)*--rice pudding.
**arroz con pollo** *(Spain)*--chicken with rice.
**asado** *(The Philippines)*--slices of beef with soy.
**asam jus** *(Indonesia)*--tamarind juice.
**atsara** *(The Philippines)*--pickled papaya.
**avgolemono** *(Greece)*--egg/lemon soup.
**ayam goreng** *(Indonesia)*--fried chicken, "Java-style".
**ayam kuri** *(Indonesia)*--chicken curry.
**ayam opor** *(Indonesia)*--chicken in coconut sauce.
**ayam rujak** *(Indonesia)*--chicken in a spicy paprika sauce.
**baba ghannouj** *(Middle East)*--smoked eggplant with olive oil.
**bacalhau** *(Portugal/Brazil)*--baked codfish.
**baghali polo** *(Persia)*--lamb shanks with lima beans, dill and saffron.
**baklava** *(Greece/Middle East/India)*--a honeyed pastry.
**bami goreng** *(Indonesia)*--fried noodles.
**bami rames** *(Indonesia)*--noodles with meats, vegetables and sauce.
**bangers and mash** *(England)*--sausages served with mashed potatoes.
**bangus** *(The Philippines)*--milkfish.
**barfi** *(India)*--a firm, flavorful cheesecake.
**barg** *(Persia)*--pounded charbroiled filet on a skewer.
**barra kabab** *(India/Persia)*--rack of lamb.
**bastani** *(Persia)*--ice cream.
**batidos de frutas** *(Cuba)*--fruit shakes.
**beef stroganoff** *(Russia)*--flambeed beef in a rich cream sauce.
**beluga ikra** *(Russia)*--black caviar.

**bengan bhartha** (*India*)--eggplant stewed in tomato curry.
**berbere** (*Ethiopia*)--combination of spices emphasizing red pepper.
**bestella** (*North Africa/Middle East*)--chicken and almonds baked in filo.
**bhajias** (*India*)--vegetables fried in garbanzo bean batter.
**bhel poori** (*India*)--a crunchy puffed cereal grain snack.
**bhindi masala** (*India*)--spiced okra in a mild masala sauce.
**bhuna gosht** (*India*)--spicy lamb curry.
**bi-bim-bab** (*Korea*)--beef and vegetables served with a fried egg on top.
**bi bim nang** (*Korea*)--cold noodles in spicy sauce.
**bife à Portuguesa** (*Portugal*)--grilled steak and eggs.
**bigos** (*Poland*)--a hunter's stew made with rabbit (Poland's national dish).
**bihon** (*The Philippines*)--rice sticks.
**bistek à la pobre** (*Peru*)--steak with fried eggs and bananas.
**blinchiki** (*Russia*)--Russian crepes.
**blini** (*Russia*)--sour dough yeast pancakes served with sour cream.
**bokumbab** (*Korea*)--fried rice.
**bolinho de bacalhau** (*Brazil*)--codfish croquette.
**borscht** (*Eastern Europe*)--beet and cabbage soup (served cold or warm).
**borek** (*Turkey*)--filo pie (*North Africa: "bourak"*).
**bratwurst** (*Germany/Switzerland*)--veal sausage.
**brik** (*North Africa*)--egg and tuna pie.
**brizoles** (*Greece*)--marinated lamb chops.
**bul-go-ki** (*Korea*)--marinated, then barbequed beef.
**camaron rebosado** (*The Philippines*)--breaded shrimps.
**camarones empanizados** (*Cuba*)--fried breaded shrimps.
**caraotas** (*Venezuela*)--black beans.
**carioca** (*Brazil*)--guava, ice cream and almonds.
**cascos de guayabas** (*Cuba*)--guava shells with cream cheese.
**cau cau** (*Peru*)--tripe.
**ceviche** (*Peru*)--fresh fish, lime, and chili.
**chai** (*India*)--spiced tea (sometimes served with milk).
**channa masala** (*India*)--garbanzo beans in a mild masala sauce.
**chapati** (*India*)--unleavened, griddle-cooked whole wheat bread.
**charuto** (*South America*)--stuffed cabbage.
**chicha morada** (*Peru*)--a popular drink made from a tasty Peruvian bean.
**chicken Kiev** (*Russia*)--breast of chicken with minced mushrooms.
**chicken korma** (*India*)--mild curried chicken with saffron
**chicken tadjin** (*North Africa*)--chicken baked with olives and mushrooms.
**chicken tikka** (*India*)--chicken baked in a tandoor with a mild sauce.
**chitcharon bulaklak** (*The Philippines*)--crisp pork innards.
**chorba m'kefta** (*North Africa*)--a hearty herb soup.
**chorizo** (*Spain*)--a spicy Spanish sausage.
**chupe de camarones** (*Peru*)--a rich soup with prawns, corn and eggs.
**churrasco** (*Argentina*)--charbroiled Argentinian steak.
**coca** (*North Africa*)--sauteed vegetables in a baked dough.

**cocos jus** (*Indonesia*)--coconut juice.
**coelho a cacadora** (*Portugal*)--traditional Portuguese rabbit stew.
**Cornish pasties** (*England*)--any of a variety of meat or vegetable pies.
**coxinha** (*Brazil*)--deep-fried chicken croquettes.
**curanto** (*Chile*)--bouillabaise.
**curry** (*India*)--a combination of spices or any sauce seasoned with same.
**curry fish noodle soup** (*Burma*)--fish, ginger, garlic, noodles and cilantro.
**dak-gu-i** (*Korea*)--chopped roast chicken.
**dal** (*India*)--cooked lentils.
**dal makhani** (*India*)--a creamy lentil curry.
**mushroom bhaji** (*India*)--mushrooms and peas in a mild curry sauce.
**dhokra** (*India*)--garbanzo bean sponge cake.
**dinuguan** (*The Philippines*)--pork in chocolate sauce.
**dobos torte** (*Hungary*)--multi-layer cake with a hard caramel crust.
**dolmades** (*Greece, Persia: dolmeh*)--grape leaves stuffed with meat.
**doogh** (*Persia*)--a lassi-like drink made from heavily salted yogurt.
**doro wat** (*Ethiopia*)--chicken simmered in spices and purified butter.
**dosas** (*South India*)--crisp ground rice and lentil crepes.
**empadinhas de queijo** (*Brazil*)--turnovers filled with cheese.
**empanada** (*Argentina, Bolivia: saltena*)--turnover stuffed with meat.
**escabeche** (*The Philippines*)--pickled halibut with ginger.
**estofado** (*The Philippines*)--beef with olives, potatoes, peppers and pickles.
**estofado de res** (*Spain*)--beef stew with red wine, onions and carrots.
**exohiko** (*Greece*)--lamb, sauteed vegetables and kasseri cheese in filo.
**falafel** (*Lebanon*)--fava beans, chick peas and spices.
**falafil** (*Burma*)--permutation of Lebanese "falafel", with split peas.
**faloodeh** (*Persia*)--an iced dessert made with tiny noodles.
**farofa** (*Brazil*)--fried yucca flour with olives, bacon and spices.
**feijoada** (*Brazil*)--smoked sausage and pork in black beans.
**fesenjun** (*Persia*)--chicken with ground walnuts in pomegranate sauce.
**flan** (*Spain, South & Central America*)--caramel custard.
**fondue** (*Switzerland*)--melted gruyere and other cheeses with bread.
**fool mandammas** (*Egypt, Middle East*)--simmered fava beans.
**frango a Brasileira** (*Brazil*)--chicken marinated in beer, then sauteed.
**frijoles negros** (*Cuba*)--black beans.
**frik** (*North Africa*)--spicy cracked wheat.
**gado-gado** (*Indonesia*)--a tomato, cucumber, egg, and peanut sauce salad.
**galatobouriko** (*Greece*)--custard topped with filo.
**gambas al ajillo** (*Spain*)--jumbo prawns grilled in garlic.
**gazpacho** (*Spain*)--the traditional Andalusian cold vegetable soup.
**ghorme sabzi** (*Persia*)--beef, herbs, red beans, onions and saffron.
**ginger salad** (*Burma*)--cabbage, peanuts, fried coconut and ginger.
**glühwein** (*Germany*)--hot, spicy mulled wine.
**golabki** (*Polish, Ukranian: golubtzy*)--stuffed cabbage.
**gomman** (*Ethiopia*)--cabbage seeds.

**gomtang** (*Korea*)--spicy beef and tripe soup.
**goon mandu** (*Korea*)--pot stickers.
**goreng** (*Indonesia*)--"fried"--at Indonesian places you'll see it often.
**goulbasi** (*Greece*)--slow cooked lamb on the shank with garlic and cheese.
**grape pula** (*Czechoslovakia*)--grape leaves stuffed with pork and paprika.
**gravalax** (*Sweden*)--smoked salmon.
**grochowka** (*Poland*)--soup made with sweet peas and ham.
**guarana** (*Brazil*)--soft drink made from a tropical fruit of the same name.
**gulab jaman** (*India*)--a rose water flavored milk ball in cardamom syrup.
**gulaman atsaya** (*The Philippines*)--agar agar with tapioca.
**gulyas** (*Hungary*)--beef and potato stew (*goulash*).
**gyros** (*Greece*)--fresh sliced roast lamb sandwiches.
**halo halo** (*The Philippines*)--shaved ice, mixed fruit and milk.
**harira** (*North Africa*)--lentil soup.
**hideg megyleves** (*Hungary*)--cold and tangy sour cherry soup.
**honguh-hweh** (*Korea*)--raw skate.
**horiatikisalta** (*Greece*)--tomato salad.
**hotobagyi palascinta** (*Hungary*)--crepes stuffed with meat.
**houmos** (Middle East)--chickpeas with lemon, olive oil and garlic.
**idli** (*South India*)--steamed rice-flour cake.
**imam baldi** (*Greece/Turkey*)--eggplant stuffed with vegetables and spices.
**injera** (*Ethiopia*)--fermented, slightly sour bread.
**Irish stew** (*Ireland*)--stew made with mutton, potatoes and onions.
**jäegerschnitzel** (*Germany*)--medallions of pork in a red sauce.
**jao jaw** (*Burma*)--coconut jello.
**jap chae** (*Korea*)--low calorie noodles.
**jerk** (*Jamaica*)--method of smoking meat or fish over an open pit.
**jhinga bhuna** (*India*)--prawns in gravy.
**jhinga tandoori** (*India*)--tandoori prawns.
**joki-gu-i** (*Korea*)--salted kingfish.
**joojeh** (*Persia*)--chicken.
**kabanocy flambe** (*Poland*)--sausages flamed in vodka.
**kachumbar** (*India*)--cucumber, tomato, onion and cilantro salad.
**kacsamaj** (*Hungary*)--chopped chicken liver.
**kal gook soo** (*Korea*)--handcut noodle soup.
**kal-bi** (*Korea*)--broiled short ribs of beef.
**kalamarakia** (*Greece*)--fried or sauteed squid.
**kalderetang** (The *Philippines*)--goat meat stew.
**kare kambing** (*Indonesia*)--lamb curry.
**kare-kare** (The *Philippines*)--ox-tail in peanut sauce.
**kartoffelsalat** (*Germany*)--homemade and usually very rich potato salad.
**käsetorte** (*Germany*)--cheesecake.
**kashko bademjan** (*Persia*)--appetizer of eggplant blended with whey.
**kassler ripchen** (*Germany*)--smoked pork loin.
**ke jang** (*Korea*)--spicy raw crab.

## GLOSSARY • 183

**kebabi(s)** (*Persia/India*)--variety of broiled meat patties.
**kecap** (*Indonesia*)--soy sauce and chili.
**keema mattar** (*India*)--minced lamb with peas, herbs and spices.
**keftethes** (*Greece*)--small meatballs.
**kheer** (*India*)--rich Indian rice pudding flavored with cardamon and nuts.
**kibbee** (*Middle East*)--cracked wheat with ground lamb and pine nuts.
**kimchee** (*Korea*)--pickled cabbage.
**kimchee-jige** (*Korea*)--pickled cabbage casserole.
**kitfo** (Ethiopia)--steak tartare.
**kofteh kebabs** (*Middle East/Persia*)--meatballs with vegetables and beans.
**koobideh** (*Persia*)--ground beef.
**kori gomtang** (*Korea*)--a spicy Korean beef and tripe soup with oxtail.
**koto lemono** (*Greece*)--chicken with lemon.
**koto kapama** (*Greece*)--sauteed chicken and vegetables in wine sauce.
**krupuk** (*Indonesia*)--shrimp toast.
**kulfi** (*India*)--homemade ice cream flavored with pistachios and almonds.
**l'ham** (*North Africa*)--lamb.
**labneh** (*Lebanon*)--cream of yogurt.
**laksa** (*Indonesia*)--a coconut-based soup with prawns and tamarind.
**lap pat doke** (*Burma*)--Burmese tea leaves, toasted lentil seeds and garlic.
**lassi** (*India*)--salty or sweet drink made with buttermilk and yogurt.
**leche flan** (The *Philippines*)--a rich milk custard.
**lengua** (The *Philippines*)--beef tongue.
**linguica** (*Portugal*)--A spicy Portuguese sausage.
**locanico** (*Greece*)--a spicy Greek sausage sometimes flavored with orange.
**lomo de cerdo** (*Spain*)--sauteed pork loin.
**lomo saltado** (*Peru*)--beef strips with vegetables and chili.
**loobia** (*Persia*)--green beans.
**lumpia** (*The Philippines*)--egg rolls with a light, crispy shell.
**makhloot** (*Persia*)--a combination of faloodeh and bastani.
**mandoo-gook** (*Korea*)--dumpling soup.
**maroulosalata** (*Greece*)--lettuce, onions, feta and kalamata olives.
**martabak** (*Indonesia*)--stuffed pancake rolls.
**mast** (*Persian*)--homemade yogurt.
**mast o khiar** (*Persia*)--yogurt with cucumbers.
**mast o musir** (*Persia*)--yogurt with shallots.
**mattar paneer** (*India*)--cubes of cheese with green peas in tomato curry.
**mechouia** (*North Africa*)--a mixed vegetable and olive oil salad.
**menudo** (*The Philippines*)--pork in tomato sauce.
**merguez** (*Tunisia*)--a lamb and beef sausage.
**mofongo** (*Cuba*)--crushed plaintains fried in garlic.
**moussaka** (*Greece*)--eggplant and ground beef baked in bechamel sauce.
**mulligatawny** (*India*)--a hearty lentil soup akin to "dal".
**muqueca de peixe** (*Brazil*)--fish in coconut broth with shrimp and nuts.
**namkeen** (*India*)--snacks.

**nan** (*India*)--unbuttered flat bread.
**nasi goreng** (*Indonesia*)--fried rice.
**nasi rames** (*Indonesia*)--fried rice topped with vegetables and meats.
**o-jin-gu-i** (*Korea*)--squid in hot sauce.
**ong no kao** (*Burma*)--coconut chicken soup.
**pabellon criollo** (*Venezuela*)--brisket of beef in a tomato sauce.
**paella Valenciana** (*Spain*)--mixed meat and seafood combination.
**paella marinera** (*Spain*)--seafood casserole.
**pakoras** (*India*)--onion fritters cooked in garbanzo bean batter.
**palascinki** (*Czechoslavakia*)--crepes suzettes.
**palascinta** (*Hungary*)--crepes.
**paluda** (*Burma*)--mixture of coconut juice, paluda syrup and ice cream.
**pancit** (*The Philippines*)--thin noodles often mixed with mung beans.
**papadum** (*India*)--a paper thin lentil wafer.
**papas a la huancaina** (*Peru*)--boiled potatoes and goat cheese.
**paratha** (*India*)--heavily-buttered, fried whole wheat bread.
**pargo** (*Spain*)--red snapper.
**parikas csirke** (*Hungary*)--chicken with paprika.
**parrillada** (*Argentina*)--traditional Argentinian "mixed grill".
**pastel** (*Brazil*)--a meat or cheese pastry.
**pasticio** (*Greece*)--pasta with meat and tomatoes.
**patra** (*India*)--steamed, then fried, taro root.
**pelimeni** (*Russia*)--Russian "ravioli" in broth.
**pergedel** (*Indonesia*)--spiced potato cakes.
**pernil de porco** (*Brazil*)--roast pork marinated in wine sauce.
**piccadillo** (*Cuba*)--ground beef "hash".
**pierogi** (*Poland*)--lightly-fried stuffed pasta shells.
**pig ear salad** (*Burma*)--pig ears with vegetables and sauce.
**Pimm's cup** (*India*)--gin sling garnished with cucumber and lemon.
**pinkabet** (*The Philippines*)--vegetables in sauce with shrimp or anchovies.
**pisang goreng** (*Indonesia*)--fried bananas.
**pitta** (*Middle East*)--flat bread.
**plombir** (*Russia*)--rich fruit ice cream.
**pollo al jerez** (*Spain*)--chicken sauted in a sherry wine sauce.
**polvo guisado** (*Portugal*)--octopus in a white wine sauce.
**poori** (*India*)--puffed and deep-fried bread.
**poulet basquaise** (*Basque Region*)--chicken and vegetables in red sauce.
**psari plaki** (*Greece*)--filet of rock cod baked in a light tomato sauce.
**pudim de coco** (*Brazil*)--coconut pudding.
**quibe** (*Brazil*)--rolled ground beef and bulgur wheat.
**quindim** (*Brazil*)--egg and coconut cupcake.
**rabo encendido** (*Cuba*)--oxtail soup.
**rahmschnitzel** (*Germany*)--veal with rushrooms in a wine cream sauce.
**raita** (*India*)--an aromatic combination of yogurt, cucumbers and spices.
**ras malai** (*India*)--Indian cheese in saffron-flavored milk with nuts.

**rassam** (*India*)--a spicy vegetable broth.
**retsina** (*Greece*)--pungent Greek "resin" wine made from pine needles.
**rijstaffel** (*Indonesia*)--multi-course Indonesian feast.
**rizogalo** (*Greece*)--rice pudding.
**ropa vieja** (*Cuba*)--shredded beef with peppers.
**rotkohl** (*Germany*)--pickled red cabbage.
**rouladen** (*Germany*)--a tender beefroll stuffed with onions and bacon.
**rujak** (*Indonesia*)--a spicy fruit and vegetable salad with peanut sauce.
**rumaki** (*Burma*)--chicken liver and waterchestnuts wrapped in bacon.
**saag paneer** (*India*)--cheese and spinach in sauce.
**sabzi** (*Persia*)--mixture of radish, mint, sweet basil and goat cheese.
**sag gosht** (*India*)--lamb cooked in a fragrant spinach sauce.
**saganiki** (*Greece*)--cheese dipped in bread crumbs and eggs, then sauteed.
**sagwala** (*India*)--spinach.
**sajur kari** (*Indonesia*)--vegetable curry.
**sajur lodeh** (*Indonesia*)--vegetables in coconut sauce.
**sajur rujak** (*Indonesia*)--vegetables in paprika sauce.
**sambar** (*India*)--thick, spicy soup similar to dal.
**samosa** (*India*)--a crisp, sometimes spicy turnover.
**samu-sa** (*Burma*)--deep-fried turnovers filled with curried potatoes.
**sandwich a la Cubane** (*Cuba*)--sandwich made of cheese, ham and pork.
**sarciado** (The *Philippines*)--spicy sauteed chunks of meat and vegetables.
**satay** (*Indonesia*)--peanut sauce.
**sauerbraten** (*Germany*)--sliced beef roasted in a marinade.
**schwarzwalder kirschtorte** (*Germany*)--black forest cherry cake.
**schweinshaxe** (*Germany*)--slowly cooked pigs knuckles.
**seekh kabab** (*India*)--minced lamb with onions and herbs on a skewer.
**seledka** (*Russia, Polish: sledz*), marinated herring.
**serundeng** (*Indonesia*)--fried coconut shreds with peanuts.
**shepherd's pie** (*England*)--a baked meat and potato casserole.
**shirin polo** (*Persia*)--chicken with orange skin, pistachios and almonds.
**shiro** (*Ethiopia*)--split pea flour in a spicy pepper sauce.
**shish tawook** (*Middle East*)--grilled chicken in lemon juice and oil.
**siopao** (The *Philippines*)--pork or chicken buns.
**sirniki** (*Russia, Poland: sernik*)--egg, sugar and cheese "pancakes".
**sirsak** (*Indonesia*)--guanabana juice.
**skorpios** (*Greece*)--sauteed prawns in a wine, feta and garlic sauce.
**sliwki** (*Poland*)--prunes rolled in hot bacon.
**sopa de mariscos** (*Spain*)--seafood soup.
**souvlakia** (*Greece*)--skewers of charbroiled, marinated meat.
**spanakopita** (*Greece*)--spinach pies baked in filo dough.
**spätzle** (*Germany*)--a small pasta sometimes substituted for potatoes.
**spotted dog** (Ireland)--spiced bread and raisin pudding, served hot.
**strudel** (*Germany*)--a light, flaky pie.
**sui gi moke** (*Burma*)--cream of wheat with poppy seeds and coconut milk.

**tabouleh** (*Lebanon*)--cracked wheat, parsley, lemon, herbs and olive oil.
**tacu tacu** (*Peru*)--rice and peas.
**tapas** (The *Philippines*)--seasoned slices of beef or pork.
**tej** (*Ethiopia*)--honey wine.
**tandoor** (*India*)--clay oven used for baking.
**tandoori** (*India*)--style of cooking where meat is cooked in a tandoor.
**taramosalata** (*Greece*)--red caviar dip.
**thali** (*India*)--a tray full of vegetarian dishes served in small metal bowls.
**tiropita** (*Greece*)--cheese pie baked in "filo" (*phylo*) dough.
**tocino** (The *Philippines*)--pork.
**tokwa't baboy** (The *Philippines*)--tofu and pork.
**toltott kaposzta** (*Hungary*)--baked stuffed cabbage.
**torshi** (*Persia*)--an appetizer of pickled vegetables.
**trucha almendrada** (*Spain*)--trout with almonds.
**turon** (The *Philippines*)--plantain bananas.
**tutu** (*Brazil*)--Fried yucca with refried beans.
**tzatziki** (*Greece*)--yogurt, cucumbers and dill.
**udang assam manis** (*Indonesia*)--sweet and sour prawns.
**utappam** (*South India*)--a thick crepe made from an onion and chili batter.
**vareniky** (*Russia*)--thin dough stuffed with farmer's cheese.
**vatapa** (*Brazil*)--seafood in peanut and coconut milk sauce.
**vindaloo** (*India*)--a hot and spicy curry sauce.
**welsh rarebit** (*U.K.*)--cheddar cheese with beer, then grilled on toast.
**wiener schnitzel** (*Germany*)--delicately breaded milk-fed veal.
**yuk-hweh** (*Korea*)--seasoned raw beef.
**zaalouk** (*Morocco*)--pureed eggplant.
**zarzuela** (*Spain*)--shellfish & fish sauted in white wine and tomato sauce.
**zereshk polo** (*Persia*)--chicken, currants and rice flavored with barberry.
**zingibel** (*Ethiopia*)--dried ginger.
**zoolbia** (*Persia*)--a sweet pastry ring, dripping with honey.

# INDEX OF RESTAURANTS

## A

Abigail's Pub, 18
Acorn, 45
Acropolis Bakery, 57
Agatha's Tea Room, 170
Alejandro's, 39, 159
Ali's, 75
Alpenrose, 177
Alpine Inn (The), 177
Alps (The), 177
Amaru, 156
Andre's Confiserie, 29
Angaare, 172
Angkor Borei, 123
Angkor Palace, 122
Angkor Wat, 169
Annalakshmi, 113
Ariana's Gourmet Food, 65
Armenian Gourmet, 69
Arooj, 108
Asmara, 170
Athens Greek, 43
Athens By Night, 43
Australian, 138
Azizi, 66

## B

B.J. Bull, 19
Baksey Cham Krong, 127
Bandidos Of The Sea, 38
Basque Cultural Center, 36
Basque Hotel, 169
Bay Bistro, 175
Bayon, 126
Beethoven, 171
Bit of England, 170
Black Forest Inn, 29
Blue Nile, 81
Bombay Cuisine, 109
Bombay Express, 112
Bombay Palace, 100
Bombaywala, 114
Britannia Arms, 170
Britannia Arms Pub, 170
Buckeye, 171
Burma, 128
Burma House, 169

## C

Cabrillo, 40
Cafe Astoria, 148
Cafe Bohemia, 55
Cafe Bombay, 98
Cafe Eritrea D'Afrique, 83
Cafe Glenda, 145
Cafe India, 172
Cafe Marmara, 66
Cafe Villa Basque, 169
Cairo Cafe, 78
Cambodian House, 169
Cambodianas (The), 126
Carinderia, 143
Carmen and Family BBQ, 167
Casablanca, 175
Casbah, 77
Caspian, 175
Catalina's, 169
Cha Cha Cha Cafe, 169
Chalet Basque, 39
Chandni, 172
Chatanoga, 175
Chelokababi, 65
Cherryland Cafe, 174
Cipriani's, 160
Copenhagen, 28
Cuba, 165
Cuban International, 163
Curry Village (The), 176

## D

Dahlak, 82
De Windmolen, 29

De Paula's, 158
Deli Eats, 70
Demitri's Deli, 172
Des Alpes, 40
Dessert Trends, 148
Don Quixote, 159
Duke of Edinburgh, 170

E

Eincr's, 170
El Amanacer, 166
El Cubane, 163
El Gallego, 38
El Greco, 172
El Mahgreb, 78
El Mansour, 175
El Morocco, 76
El Nuevo Frutilandia, 165
El Oso, 35
El Patio, 36
El Tumi, 158
Embassy, 173
English Rose, 16
English Tea Shop, 20
Ensenada, 167
Eugene's, 54
Eunice's, 157
European Deli, 175

F

Filipinas, 149
Filipino Merienda, 171
Fina Estampa, 157
Finn McCool's, 174
Fondue Fred's, 30
Fono Paprikas, 55
Francesca's, 159

G

Ganges (The), 99
Gasthaus, 172
Gaylord, 96, 103, 110-112
Gelco's, 56

German Cook, 26
German Oak, 28
Geva's, 169
Gita's, 107, 173
Gold Ribbon Bake Shop, 171
Golden Duck Grill, 169
Goldilocks, 146
Govinda's, 114
Grapeleaf (The), 174
Greco-Romana Pizzeria, 172
Greek Islands Delights, 172
Guernica, 169
Gypsy Cellar (The), 52

H

Habibi, 174
Haig's Delicacies, 69
Han Il Kwan, 146
Heart of Europe, 170
Henry VIII, 170
Himalaya, 109
Hochburg Von Germania, 25
House Of Prime Rib, 20
Hungarian Huszar (The), 54
Hungarian Restaurant, 172

I

Iberia Restaurant, 39
India Cafe (The), 97
India Garden, 113
India House, 103
India Kashmir, 106
India Mahal, 173
India Oven, 173
India Palace Restaurant, 104
India Pavillion, 110
Indonesia, 145
Ireland's 32, 19
J & J Philippine, 149
Java, 147
Jawad Cafe & Deli, 174
Jin-Go-Gae, 147
Jose's, 167
Just Like Home, 68

## K

Kabab Cafe, 173
Kabab House, 176
Kabila, 173
Kabul, 68
Kasra Persian Cuisine, 69
Kenkoy's Diner, 142
Kensington Circus, 19
Khayyam's Chelo Kabab, 64
Khyber India, 173
King Se-Jong, 143
Korean Bar-B-Que, 174
Korean Cabin, 142
Korean Corner, 149
Korea House, 148, 174
Korean Palace, 174
Korean Restaurant, 147
Korean Secret Garden, 147

## L

La Belle Creole 162
La Bodega, 176
La Roca, 176
La Santaneca (de la M.) 166
Lan Xang, 125
Las Cazuelas, 175
Las Palmeras, 165
Las Tinajas, 164
Lippizaner, 30
Little Bavaria, 172
Little Copenhagen, 170
Little Spain, 176
Liverpool Lil's, 170
London House, 17
Los Cocos, 176
Lucerne, 177
Luzern, 177

## M

Mabuhay House, 171
Maharani, 112
Mamonluk, 171
Mamounia (2), 175
Mandalay, 124
Manila Bay, 171
Manila Express, 171
Manssur's, 175
Marrakech Palace, 175
Massawa, 170
Matterhorn, 27
Max's Fried Chicken, 171
Mayflower Inne, 17
Maykadeh, 67
Mediterranean Gardens, 70
Mela, 173
Menara, 175
Middle East, 67
Mike's XLNT Foods, 46
Milvia, 144
Miracle Mile Cafe, 70
Misha's Russian Cafe, 176
Mister Go, 171
Mother India, 111
Morning Star (The), 44
Mumtaj, 173
Mykonos Restaurant, 46

## N

Nan Yang, 125
Nayang Pilipino, 170
New Delhi, 173
New Delhi Junction, 111
Nicaragua, 164
Niki's, 172
Nino's, 160
Noble Pies, 149
Nordic Gourmet Kafe, 28
Norman's, 176
North India, 102
Nusrat Sweets, 173
Nyala's, 84

## O

Obrero Hotel 169
Old Swiss House, 27
Oliver Ritz, 148
On Lok Yuen, 128

Ori-Deli, 174
Orient Express, 175

P

Pacific Breeze, 171
Pacific Sunset, 171
Padang, 139
Palace Korean, 174
Panos, 45
Papa's, 69
Paradise, 176
Pars, 176
Pasand, 106-114
Pasha, 175
Patusco's, 40
Payumo's, 146
Peacock Restaurant, 105
Pelican Inn, 16
Penny Farthing, 20
Penny Farthing Pub, 18
Perogies Please, 57
Petrouchka, 56
Philippine (The), 139
Philippine Gourmet, 171
Phnom Penh, 128
Phnom Penh House, 127
Pit Cozy, 176
Po Seok Chung, 140
Prince Of Wales, 20
Prince Neville, 174

R

Rasselas, 85
Red Sea, 82
Red Balloon, 175
Rice Table (The), 137
Royal India, 105, 115
Royal Morocco, 175
Royal Taj, 173
Russian Renaissance, 53

S

S. Asimakopoulos Cafe, 44

Sabina, 104, 173
Sahrang Bahng, 141
Salonika, 44
Sam Da Do, 174
Satay House, 174
Sayeed Kababs, 110
Sayonn's, 128
Scandinavian Deli, 175
Schroeder's Cafe, 26
Sea Cliff, 172
Seoul, 174
Seoul Garden, 144
Seoul House, 145
Seven Ports, 172
Shaikh's India Foods, 113
Sheba Restaurant, 84
Shish Mahal, 173
Silva's, 37
Sinugba, 171
Sorabol, 140
Sousa's, 39
Speckmann's, 25
Stanley's, 15
Stoyanof's, 45
Sue's Kitchen, 95
Sujatha's, 113, 115
Sulo Filipino, 171
Sultan (The), 175
Sunrise Deli, 68
Sweden House, 29
Swedish Place, 177
Sweet Sensations, 171
Swiss Alps, 177

T

Taj Kesri, 108
Tamar, 37
Tandori, 114
Tambo, 160
Tango, 176
Taste of India, 173
Taverna Athena, 172
Teasara, 176
Teske's Germania, 27
Tito Rey, 141

## V

Verona, 45
Vicki's Place, 57
Village Green, 170
Vladimir's, 53
Vlasta's, 56
Volga, 57

## W • Y • Z

Welcome Mat, 166
Wild Strawberry, 170
Yas Cafe, 70
Zula Restaurant, 83

## ORDER FORM

Please send me ( ) copy(ies) of A Guide to The Bay Area's Best Ethnic Restaurants (1990 Edition). I enclose $14.95 ($12.95 plus tax and postage) for each copy ordered.

My name_____

Address_____

City/State/Zip Code_____

Send as a gift to:_____

Address_____

City/State/Zip Code_____

**SEND TO:** ZORBA PRESS WEST P.O. BOX 8224 BERKELEY CA 94707